The Dual-Credit Phenomenon!

Challenging Secondary School Students Across 50 States

By Hans A. Andrews

NEW FORUMS PRESS INC.

Stillwater, Oklahoma U.S.A.

This book may be ordered in bulk quantities at discount
from New Forums Press, Inc., P.O. Box 876, Stillwater, OK
74076 [Federal I.D. No. 73 1123239]. Printed in the United
States of America.

International Standard Book Number: 1-58107-044-6

Contents

Preface

The Dual-Credit movement in secondary schools in cooperation with community college and senior college and university support is becoming a revolutionary phenomenon. It is reaching hundreds of thousands of secondary school students who are ready for an advanced program of study prior to leaving high school.

This book is a labor of love that I wish to share with the many good people who have taken on the challenge of providing the dual-credit option to secondary school students across the country. It is also dedicated to those who will be part of this important movement in the years ahead.

Dual-credit programs and course offerings accelerate the start of college for those who are ready. They provide the general education offerings that are almost universal in American community colleges and universities. Many programs have also attracted secondary schools to enroll students into the technical and vocational offerings of the community colleges.

This writer has been involved in some form of the dual-credit movement since the mid-1960s. As the Director of Guidance I had the support of the high school principal at Lowell High School, Michigan, to allow some of our students to obtain dual-credit course credit from Grand Rapids Junior College in Michigan. Welding and introductory manufacturing courses kept some of my most difficult students interested in staying in school.

Marquette High School and Seneca High School in the northern half of Illinois provided some of us at Illinois Valley Community College with a "live laboratory" to show what could be accomplished between a community college and secondary schools. Students were able to earn from 12 to 30 semester hours of dual-credit during a two-year period while finishing high school.

This program began in 1985 and has proven to be an outstandingly successful endeavor for the students who were encouraged to enroll. Not one student over the years has come back to complain about the quality of the program. A significant number were able to shorten their time for completing a baccalaureate degree to three years. Research in 1990 and again in 2000 found exceptional support from alumni of this dual-credit program for continuing the effort.

Special thanks go to my colleague, Dr. Robert Marshall, Vice President of Student Services at Illinois Valley Community College (IVCC), for the tremendous support he gave to supporting and developing this program at a time when it was new in the state of Illinois. Robert never let the doubters on campus, off campus, or around the state deter him from moving the effort forward. The division chairpersons at IVCC did an exceptional job of staffing the program as well as evaluating it and assuring quality instruction for the students. Special thanks also goes to Jackie Davis, Dean of Instruction at my present college. He has provided strong leadership in making dual-credit a substantial program with a number of secondary schools located in our college district.

I am grateful for the leadership of Joan Jobst, former principal of Marquette High School, Ottawa, Illinois, and Harlen "Butch" Cotter, former superintendent of Seneca High School, Illinois, and now superintendent of Robinson High School in Illinois, for their support and dedication to this program. Thanks to them, it is one of the original outstanding models in the Midwest from 1985 forward.

Dual-credit programs for high school students should become the number-one educational revolution in the country as the new century gets underway. It is pulling the K-12 system together with higher education institutions throughout the country. It is a program that will challenges honor students as well as other students seeking a challenge in technology careers.

The program will prove to be very cost effective for state legislative bodies. The time-to-degree concerns of the 1990s should be relieved to a large degree. Student motivation will be enhanced as has been seen in the many school districts that utilize this pro-

---

gram with their students. Those secondary school teachers who have the responsibility of preparing students for the last two years of high school should find themselves under a certain amount of pressure to prepare their students for this new and expanded challenge.

Special thanks goes to my wife, Carolyn, who has given me her support during the several months of this project.

The Author

HANS A. ANDREWS is President of Olney Central College in Southeastern Illinois. He has a Bachelor of Science degree (1960) in Business Education from Central Michigan University. He received a Master of Arts degree in Counseling and Guidance in 1963 from Michigan State University. In 1971 he earned his Ed.D. degree in Counseling Psychology and Higher Education Administration from the University of Missouri-Columbia.

Andrews' professional roles in community colleges have been primarily in administration. He was Dean of Instruction at Illinois Valley Community College, and Vice President for Community and Student Services at Kellogg Community College. That position was preceded by the positions of Dean of Community Services, Evening College Dean, and Evening College Counselor, also at Kellogg Community College. These positions were preceded by five years of high school teaching and roles as Director of Counseling and Guidance in two secondary schools. Dr. Andrews also taught part-time as an adjunct instructor in the Department of Curriculum and Instruction at Illinois State University.

Over the past 30 years Andrews has published three books, *Evaluating for Excellence, Merit in Education* and *Teachers Can Be Fired: The Quest for Quality.* In addition, he has written several chapters in educational books, published over 70 professional articles and served on three editorial boards of educational journals. He has conducted several studies on faculty evaluation practices in American community colleges and has consulted with over 100 community colleges to assist them in improving evaluation of faculty.

Foreword

THIS BOOK SHOULD CARRY A SPECIAL LABEL: "WARNING – *Reading may cause other advance placement programs to become obsolete!"*

Hans Andrews has gathered into his volume an impressive array of plans, programs, outlines and lessons for secondary and college administrators, counselors, and parents. Where these plans have been implemented, they have created exceptional learning partnerships.

My friend Hans is not an educational faddist, taking the latest theory and puffing it to today's must-have hula hoop. No, there are educators, and then there are EDUCATORS. Hans is a practitioner. My own thirty-two years of experience in education have allowed me to tell the difference between the two, and I have been given the opportunity to work side-by-side with EDUCATORS who create climates where exceptional learning opportunities are available to students.

This book, *The Dual-Credit Phenomenon*, is about such opportunities.

Whether writing about programs he has created in mid-western communities and rural areas, or chronicling the work of others, Hans is as lucid as he is practical about dual-credit.

Make no mistake. Dual-credit is a powerful idea. What student would not jump at the opportunity to earn that first year of college credits with little or no expense while completing the final years of high school?

If our students are to be prepared academically and financially for post-secondary experiences, dual-credit opportunities

---

must be made more available. This book contains the resources to help us meet the high expectations of our parents and of our nation.

As the world continues to shrink to one global village, the future will belong to the educated. The leading schools will be those that take full advantage of high school and college resources and have the courage to use those resources by implementing dual-credit partnerships.

Harlen "Butch" Cotter
Superintendent
Robinson Community Unit No. 2
206 S. Jackson
Robinson, IL 62454

To Carolyn

...Who has stayed strong for me in sickness and in health.

I.

Acceleration is a well-researched, desirable option that improves achievement for gifted students (Benbow & Lupinski, 1996). Yet, it is rarely a solution chosen by schools (Jones & Southern, 1989). If we let your child learn the next grade level curriculum now, what will we teach him or her next year? Neither teacher nor parent finds tolerable the image of a 12th grader, or even occasionally a younger student, sitting through a year of school with nothing to learn. The most acceptable remedy has been to dole it out at a pace too slow for bright students (McCarthy, 1999).

Dual-Credit: A 21st Century Phenomenon

Why should a high school senior have to spend his or her last year in high school *"blowing off the senior year?"* This is an expression used by many high school seniors across America in recent years. It is an expression that highlights the fact that large numbers of seniors, and a significant number of juniors, have completed all or most of the required college level preparatory classes that their schools have to offer and now can coast through to the final destination of graduation with few challenges left.

Botstein (2001) stated that, "the majority of college-bound seniors admit that their final year of high school is a waste of time. Increasingly, that criticism is being leveled at the last two years (p. 25)." He sees the need for high schools to replace the junior high school in order to focus on 13 to 16 year olds. Those at age 16, according to Botstein, would take their high school diploma and choose to attend a community college or a four-year college or start work, internships, or perhaps some form of national service.

Conley depicts seniors as suffering from "senioritis" in their last year of high school. Seniors, according to his analysis, see the last half of the senior year as a time they have earned and do little as their reward. He predicts that, while the high school in the United States is not going to end, it is, indeed, going to change (p. 10).

In what might be described as an indictment report on the senior year of high school, the *National Commission on the High School Senior Year* (2001) found that there has been little interconnection between the K-12 and postsecondary education systems. The Commission saw them as acting independently of each other. The senior year was described as a fairly lost cause for many seniors:

> For a variety of reasons, student motivation drops in the senior year. Short of a miserable failure in the senior year, practically every college-bound student knows that what they have accomplished through grade 11 will largely determine whether or not they attend college, and if so, which college. As a result, serious preparation ends at Grade 11 (p. 6).

One of the commission's co-chairpersons, Dr. Jacquelyn M. Belcher, announced that they found that, while the economy and workforce were changing at lightning speed, many of the colleges, and secondary schools, were standing still—basically doing the same thing for the past quarter of a century (p.1). She suggested that a seamless passage is needed in every phase of education. She referred to her own community college, Georgia Perimeter College, as having over 900 students enrolled in a dual enrollment program to help ease the transition from high school to college. It is the largest program in Georgia.

This state of affairs has dramatically changed for high school students during the last years of the 20th Century and leading into the 21st Century. Enlightened secondary school administrators, community college leaders, and some innovative university people have developed a new and challenging program entitled *dual-credit* or *dual enrollments or concurrent enrollment.*

During a meeting of the *Education Commission of the States*, Ted Sanders, president of the commission, called for the creation of entities in the states to share the decision-making over those issues that are affecting both higher education and the public school system. He said, "we need joint power, not just talk." At that same meeting Tom Vander Ark, executive director for education for the Bill and Melinda Gates Foundation exclaimed, "the large, comprehensive American high school is a disaster ... it doesn't work for most kids (Basinger, 2000)."

Puyear (1998) identified four current issues that arise from the community college literature and from his discussions with other community college state directors, and others at the national level. He sees these as the same four issues that are also being dealt with in state legislatures across the United States:

(1) Transfer articulation;
(2) Distant education;
(3) Remedial education; and
(4) Concurrent enrollment of high school students in community college courses.

In the state of Arizona the law requires the State Board and the Arizona Board of Regents to adopt rules to require community colleges to admit students under the age of eighteen who have not yet attained a high school diploma. Puyear refers to the Arizona statute requiring each school district having to make this information available to all students in at least grades nine through twelve.

The number of students enrolled, as well as types of courses and programs offered must be reported each year to the President of the Senate, the Speaker of the House of Representatives, and the State Board of Education.

These requirements are similar to the types of legislative mandates in Washington, Missouri, Virginia, and several other states as their programs are developing and expanding.

Who would have dreamed that prior to the turn of the 21st Century our secondary school system would move much closer to a merger with the higher education system in America? The search for meaningful and timely education has plagued secondary school boards, superintendents, and principals for a long time.

High schools had, over the years, developed *honors classes* to keep their brightest students challenged. They had also sent some of their faculty members for training in order to offer the *Advanced Placement (AP)* college course equivalency program of the College Board. The AP program offered them up to 33 courses in 19 subject areas. The year 2000 found 1.2 million AP exams being administered to over 750,000 students around the world through 13,000 secondary schools (The College Board, 2001).

Some secondary schools had also been benefitting by being located in cities and towns near universities and/or community colleges. The proximity to colleges allowed a number of the schools to release some students to take college classes during the normal school day hours or during the evenings and weekends.

The Movement Into Dual-Credit

During the last two decades of the 20th Century a new and most significant movement was starting. It has become known as the *dual-credit* program movement. The program has been in place in some parts of the country over the past 25 to 40 years. In recent years the interest and delivery of programs has started to peak.

The dual-credit program has allowed juniors and seniors to obtain college credit. Secondary schools have allowed the students to use that same credit as part of their secondary school graduation requirements. A number of universities and four-year colleges across the nation have also developed dual-credit or concurrent enrollment programs. The most significant growth recently, however, has been in the community college systems across the country.

State educational coordinating agencies, community colleges, and universities have worked closely with their state legislators to develop supportive legislation, funding, standards for delivery, and guarantees for transferability of these dual-credit programs to universities and colleges across the state and nation.

Definitions: Dual-Credit and Concurrent Enrollment

There is confusion as to what is meant by *dual-credit* and *concurrent enrollment* of secondary school students. Many people use the terms interchangeably. For purposes of this book, and for the reader, the two types of enrollment definitions are as follows:

Dual-Credit Students: These are secondary school students en-rolled in college credit classes who receive both college credit _and_ credit toward meeting secondary school requirements for graduation.Some courses are used to replace required courses for high school graduation and others are used as electives to-ward the same graduation.

Concurrent Enrolled Students: This term is used to describe high school students enrolled in college courses for credit while continuing to be enrolled as high school students and being counted in Average Daily Membership at the high school (Andrews, 2000-2001). It involves those college courses where _only_ college credit is obtained and such credit is not used for high school credit (Puyear, 1998).

Concurrent enrolled students are enrolled in college for some courses while still enrolled at their home high school. There are, and will be, differences of opinion on these two definitions. The reader, however, should find that these definitions are used as con-sistently as possible throughout this book. There will be programs, however, described that use concurrent enrollments to describe what this author has just identified as dual-credit programs. These will be pointed out in subsequent chapters.

Models for Dual-Credit and Concurrent Enrollment

There have been several dual-credit models developed over the years, some from legislation and others from practice and ex-perience in a number of states. Puyear suggests six _possible_ mod-els have been evolving in the Arizona Community College system:

1. The course is taught as an augmentation of a high school course.
2. A high school teacher teaches the course and it is taught at the high school during the school day.
3. The course is taught at the high school during the school day,

but the teacher is a community college teacher who is not also a high school teacher.

4. The course is taught at a location other than the high school, but it is limited to high school concurrent enrollment students.

5. The course is taught at a location other than the high school and high school students are mixed with college students.

6. Some other arrangement as described by individual college district and secondary schools.

Puyear's models provide a good summary of the options of how dual-credit courses are offered. They are consistent with what this author has found in programs throughout the United States.

A recently formed national group has begun providing an outlet for professionals working with concurrent enrollment programs. The *National Alliance of Concurrent Enrollment Partnerships (NACEP)* now has its own website which also links it to a number of its member colleges. This alliance is designed to, "link college-school programs offering college courses in high schools." In addition, it offers these other benefits:

> NACEP supports and promotes its constituent programs through quality initiatives, program development, national standards, research, and communication (Website: "http://supa.syr.edu/nacep/" p. 1).

This national alliance appears to be the only such group formed relative to dual-credit and/or concurrent enrollment programs. Its movement toward developing national standards, quality initiatives and research can only enhance and strengthen the dual-credit movement.

Benefits of Dual-Enrollment Programs

There have been a significant number of studies that have identified benefits of dual-enrollment programs for secondary school students. The Oregon *Early Options* program is one of them and the following benefits have been defined (Oregon University System, 1999):

- Acceleration of progress for students
- Reduced tuition costs for students and parents
- Reassurance for parents concerning their children's ability to handle college-level academic responsibilities
- Relief of high school boredom
- Productive interaction between high schools and colleges
- Facilitated student recruitment
- Enhanced college-community relations
- Opportunities to address equity concerns (social equity)

Each of these benefits offers strong support for the dual-credit program. They offer motivational reasons for students as well. Improved cooperation between secondary schools and higher education institutions is no small accomplishment or benefit.

"I've seen students who no one thought had much talent, but then later in college they just connected and blossomed," was Levin's way of expressing his support for utilizing community colleges to help motivate underachieving students at the secondary school level. Levin continued, "the problem is motivation; for a lot of kids, schools are boring and school devalued" (Lords, 2000, p.2). Levin is the founding director of a program in Vermont called *Accelerated Schools Project.*

Lords reported that the enrollment in Vermont's 13 campuses of the Community College of Vermont's program had grown from 90 to 210 in less than the two years since the program opened in 1998. Levin made a plea for financial support by pointing out that many of the parents of students who should be in this program are not able to provide the college tuition of $400 per each three credit hour course in the Community College of Vermont program.

Time-to-Degree Concerns

One of the prevailing concerns at the beginning of the 21st Century has been the length of time it takes students to arrive at a baccalaureate degree. Many full-time students take between 4.5 to

5.5 years to complete the degree. In Illinois an *Affordability Study Committee* pushed for options for students in the secondary schools as part of the solution to reducing the time-to-degree. One of their options was an accelerated program for students who are academically ready.

Legislation to support dual-credit funding and tuition reduction or replacement was added to the Illinois Community College system soon after the *Affordability Study Committee* published its report. It is similar to legislation now offered in a number of other states (Affordability Committee, 1996).

Program Titles

There are a number of titles that have been developed to describe the dual-credit and concurrent enrollment programs. Some of them are *Concurrent Enrollment* (Utah), *Kansas Challenge to Secondary School Pupils Act*, *Running Start* (New Hampshire, Nevada, Washington), *Fast Start* (New Jersey), *Post-Secondary Enrollment Options* (Ohio, Idaho,), *Postsecondary Dual-Credit Program (PSDCP)* (Georgia) and *Post-Secondary Education Options Program (WPEOP)* (Wyoming).

Other states have similar titles or have the programs listed under a series of secondary school enrollment option programs in state legislation.

Tuition Charges

The charging of college tuition for dual-credit courses varies from state to state. In some states, such as Illinois, the state has provided a tuition replacement fund for community colleges. This fund is known as the *Accelerated College Enrollment Grant* and reimburses the colleges so they can either waive the tuition or significantly reduce it. The Education Commission of the States identified programs in Colorado, Florida, Georgia, Maine, Massachusetts, Michigan, Minnesota, New Jersey, Ohio, Utah, Washington, and Wisconsin having comprehensive programs in which students pay little or no tuition.

In some states the secondary schools are given funding that goes either to pay for the tuition or is paid directly to the colleges for tuition charges encountered. The states of Arizona, Arkansas, Indiana, Kansas, Louisiana, and North Dakota were identified as having students paying for the tuition charges.

It was suggested by Boswell that legislators consider funding the dual or concurrent enrollment of high school juniors and seniors in community college courses and provide incentives to them to accelerate their educational advancement (2000). She pointed out that Utah offers students who earn associate degrees within a three-month period following high school graduation a scholarship from the state to cover 75% of their tuition and fees for upper-division coursework taken at state institutions.

The Growth and Need for Research

The growth in dual-credit enrollments has been exceptionally high over the past few years. As funding from the state has improved to support both the community college and university systems, the outreach has been expanded greatly by the colleges. The ability to offer dual-credit courses in some states at no tuition or at a reduced tuition cost has encouraged many more students to get involved in this option.

How successful are these dual-credit students? The preliminary research results that have been published indicate that the dual-enrollment programs are achieving their goals and students are reporting success as they move further into their degree work after high school graduation. There is, however, a need for much more research in each of the states to document the successes and impact of dual-credit programs on their students. Several surveys from former students giving positive testimonial support of the programs have been documented. Much more is needed. The accomplishments of students enrolled in universities and community colleges needs to show time-to-degree being shortened as well as continuing success of students in subsequent coursework. Shortcomings of dual-credit programs also need to be identified so programs can continue to make quality improvements.

Quality Control

The need for guaranteeing quality in dual-credit programs is paramount. There will be references made throughout this book that dual-credit will only survive when students are given a high level of instruction in each and every dual-credit course in which they enroll. We must stay vigilant on this issue. It is our *number one concern*. No matter how much public support and funding is forthcoming for dual-credit programs, quality teaching continues to be the number one guarantee needed.

Summary

The dual-credit movement in American secondary schools and colleges has expanded dramatically. This author has referred to this movement as a *phenomenon* which can be defined as an extraordinary event or happening.

Dual-credit programming has caught the imagination of educators, legislators, governing boards, parents and students throughout the country. Legislators and governors have found these programs to be some of the most rewarding new programs to answer their concerns relative to (1) secondary school challenges; (2) cost of education in higher education; and (3) time-to-degree. Parents and students are demanding these programs be offered, expanded, and of a high enough quality that transfer of credit will not be a problem.

It is important to note that the dual-credit development is so dynamic that the growth, funding patterns, enrollment options, and tuition agreements are changing rapidly. It is like trying to hit a moving target to attempt to report on which states are doing what in dual-credit at any given time.

The fact that the dual-credit program has emerged at the turn of the 21st Century is interesting. It could well be the program that will be highlighted as one of the major 21st Century events in the improvement of education.

II.

In June of 1998, 20 Running Start *students graduated with their Associate of Arts Degree from Clark College. These same graduates were also graduating with their high school diploma at the same time (*Reisberg, 1998*).*

Dual-Credit: *State Plans*

The dual-credit movement has been a quiet movement for a number of colleges and secondary school districts over the years. Individual colleges have had arrangements with secondary schools within their districts that have allowed students to enroll in specific college courses with the approval of the high school superintendent, principal or counselor and parents for several decades. It has only been in recent years that state governments have developed a strong interest in this option for challenging secondary school students.

The dual-credit movement is part of the answer to the critics of secondary school education. It is one of the programs developed to challenge students during the final two years of high school. It also provides outlets for those students interested in the more technical education fields. In addition, it is answering some of the concerns of legislators and educational leaders relative to the time and cost it has been taking students to complete their baccalaureate degrees. This author sees the following positive outcomes of dual-credit programs:

(1) Secondary schools, community colleges and universities are working together and providing college level courses for students who are ready for early entry into college work;

---

(2) Students are leaving high school with one-semester or one-year of college work completed; others are completing an Associate Degree by the end of their high school years;

(3) There has been very little difficulty in transferring college dual-credit courses to higher education institutions;

(4) Students in follow-up studies have reported that the courses have been as challenging or more challenging than those courses subsequently taken at the university.

State Interest in dual-credit programs

Dual-credit offerings have been documented as being offered by individual junior and community colleges as early as the 1950s but have only recently been looked at by states (Girardi and Stein, 2000). Legislation and procedures and approval of such programs by state educational bodies have added greatly to the legitimacy of this program's thrust.

Oregon's Joint Boards of Education commissioned a study of current policies and practices across the country in 1997. A total of 31 states responded as having some type of dual-credit program.

Fourteen states reported having specific laws or policies addressing early options programs such as dual-credit. They were: Arizona, Colorado, Florida, Georgia, Idaho, Indiana, Iowa, Michigan, Minnesota, North Dakota, Ohio, Oklahoma, Virginia, and Washington.

This same study identified 23 of the states responding as having programs with (1) dual enrollment (high school and college), (2) concurrent enrollment, and/or (3) dual-credit. A number of other states pointed out that they offered secondary school students the Advanced Placement (AP) program, CLEP, Dante Challenge Exam, or some other postsecondary options. The following is a state-by-state listing summarized by an *Oregon Early Options Study Committee*:

State-by-State Listing of High School – College Credit Programs*

Alabama - State Board of Education has a policy on this for two-year colleges
Arkansas - Dual-credit is permitted by state law
Colorado - State offers Postsecondary Enrollment Options
Connecticut - Community colleges and University have separate programs
Florida - State offers Advanced Placement and dual-enrollment
Georgia - State offers Postsecondary Enrollment Options and Joint Enrollment
Idaho - State offers Advanced Placement and dual-enrollment programs
Illinois - Programs offered, especially through community colleges
Iowa - State offers Postsecondary Enrollment Options
Kentucky - State offers dual-credit programs
Maryland - State offers concurrent enrollment programs
Massachusetts - State offers dual-enrollment programs
Minnesota - State offers Postsecondary Enrollment Options
Mississippi - State offers Advanced Placement programs
Missouri - State offers Advanced Placement and dual-enrollment programs
Montana - State offers Advanced Placement, CLEP, and Dante challenge exams
Nebraska - State offers support for Advanced Placement and dual-enrollment
Nevada - State has implemented a new distance education initiative
New Mexico - State funds concurrent enrollment and Advanced Placement exam fees
North Carolina - State supports Advanced Placement
North Dakota - State offers Advanced Placement and dual-credit enrollment programs
Ohio - State offers Postsecondary Enrollment Options program
Oklahoma - State supports concurrent enrollment and Advanced Placement
Oregon - Individual campuses may offer college classes to high school students
South Carolina - Institutions may offer college courses at high schools
South Dakota - State offers dual-enrollment and Advanced Placement programs
Texas - State law provides for dual-credit
Utah - State supports concurrent enrollment
Virginia - State encourages dual-enrollment, dual-credit, & Advanced Placement
Washington - State offers Running Start and College in the High School programs
West Virginia - A policy is under development; individual systems have had programs
Wisconsin - State encourages Advanced Placement and Postsecondary options
Wyoming - State offers dual-concurrent enrollment programs

California, Hawaii, Indiana, Kansas, Maine, Michigan, New Hampshire, New York, Pennsylvania, Rhode Island, Tennessee, reported programs existed but did not provide any supporting data.

Source: State Higher Education Executive Officers (1998). Statewide College Admissions, Student Preparation, and Remediation Policies and Programs, Boulder, Colorado

The above responses represent 44 states having some type of postsecondary options for students available. Reisberg (1998) reported thirty-eight states had been identified as having formal dual-credit programs.

Updated State Information

This author has extended his research during 2000 and 2001 to include all of the remaining states. All 50 states now have materials available for this book on the status of dual-credit and/or dual enrollment programming. Some of the materials were made available from contacts at Community College State Coordinating Boards. Other materials were found by searching the Internet. A number of individual colleges were found listing their dual-credit, dual enrollment, or concurrent program in their home pages. Some colleges were sent questionaires from this researcher.

All 50 states have now responded and all but two have indicated that there is some active dual-credit or concurrent course work by secondary schools underway in those states. There appears to be additional pressure mounting to offer these programs in those remaining states.

Program Titles

The dual-credit and concurrent enrollment programs challenging secondary school students have taken on a number of titles. Some of these are:

Colorado has a *Fifth-Year High School Program for Advanced Students.* Idaho lists its programs under their *Postsecondary Enrollment Options.* The Kansas program is known as the *Kansas Challenge to Secondary School Pupils Act.* Massachusetts included their program under the *Education Reform Act of 1993.*

The state of Michigan program, under its *Postsecondary Enrollment Options Act Update,* was expanded in 1999. Minnesota has provided options for secondary school students since 1985 through their *Post-Secondary Enrollment Options Act.* In New Jersey accelerated student learning came under *The Higher Education Restructuring Act in 1996.* Syracuse University, within the state of New York, has promoted a program for advanced high school students since 1979 under the title of *Project Advance.*

In 1990 New Mexico strengthened its concurrent enrollment policy within their *Policies Governing Concurrent Enrollment of*

Secondary Students at Postsecondary Institutions. Ohio expanded options for juniors and seniors in their *Post-Secondary Enrollment Options Program.* The state of Wyoming, since 1995, has had a concurrent enrollment program under their *Wyoming Postsecondary Education Options Program.* The program designated in the state of Washington to handle advanced student enrollments is *Running Start.* Delaware has a *School-to-Work Career Pathway* program.

In communications that I received from Sandra Edmunds, Pennsylvania Department of Education, Bureau of Secondary Services, it was clearly stated that Pennsylvania does have a statewide policy for public community colleges that currently *excludes* in-school youth. There was nothing to indicate that this was under review or any changes would be considered in the immediate future.

Vincennes University (a two-year community college in Indiana) has been promoting a concurrent enrollment program under *Project Excel* for 25 years. The courses are offered in Indiana high schools. Content, assignments, grading standards and textbooks meet the same standards as the Vincennes University on-campus courses. The college department chairs work on the approval of these requirements.

Senior level high school standing is required for this program. Some exceptions, however, are allowed through a process approval review with the Project EXCEL coordinator.

A student may enroll in up to 12 semester hours a semester. Any request for more hours will be considered through an appeals process with the coordinator of the program. Faculty must meet the North Central Association credential requirements for associate degree teaching.

The Ivy Tech State College system in Indiana is in the process of becoming the Community College of Indiana. Up to this time they have offered dual-credit classes throughout the state. Each of their regional campuses offers the option of secondary school students receiving college credit for approved vocational/career program offerings. The plan is to expand these agreements significantly in the next few years. As the Ivy Tech system gains full comprehensive community college status it is expected that dual-credit offerings will be made available to students in the general education subjects.

Evolving Programs

Vermont

Vermont, at the time of this publication, has legislation being considered for dual enrollment programs. It was described as a "hot topic" by Mindy Boenning, Community College of Vermont (CCV), in correspondence with this author. The CCV has 12 sites in Vermont as it is a statewide institution. It has developed the *Rise to the Challenge* program for high school students.

There is no coordinating policy in Vermont or dual enrollment support from the state. The only students who can participate at this time with CCV are those who can afford the $431 tuition for a three credit hour class.

Ms. Boenning indicated that CCV had 26 schools interested in 2001 in developing dual enrollment programs with them. Most of them have been unable to find the funding to assist students with this program. CCV is collaborating with the Governor's appointed High School Task Force which has dual enrollment in its top ten priorities. CCV is very optimistic that the need, interest, and motivation is there to initiate the program in the near future.

Maryland

The state of Maryland had dual enrollment legislation passed and signed by the governor in House Bill 1127 in April, 2001. This legislation provides the following:

1. A funding mechanism to permit qualified high school students to enroll at community colleges while still in high school;
2. Funds would be available to create a matching scholarship or waiver awarded by a community college to a high school student;
3. This would enhance the senior year of many high school students who have completed a majority of their high school requirements and are waiting for graduation (Maryland Association of Community Colleges).

House Bill 1127 also calls for those postsecondary institutions that participate in the program to establish criteria to award grants or waivers for the dual enrolled students. This program now shows promise of large growth.

Chesapeake College in Maryland charges only 50 percent of the tuition for their dual enrollment students. In a public information release in June of 2001 they announced:

> Sherye Hathaway, a senior at North Caroline High School, decided to enroll as a full-time college student this year through the Dual Enrollment program to accumulate enough credits to attend St. Mary's College in Maryland as a transfer student in Fall 2001 Semester (Molloy, p. 1).

Sherye Hathaway's mother, Evie Hathaway, remarked, "the dual enrollment program was a wonderful experience for my daughter. It matured her as a person and she learned a lot. I encourage parents to inquire about the program (p. 1)." Mrs. Hathaway has a second daughter who will be entering the program. It is a program open to both juniors and seniors. Chesapeake College's PR release also announced that one of their dual enrollment students had completed his Associate's Degree at the same time he graduated from his high school. Vicky Wilson, a counselor at Easton High School was also quoted in the Public Information release saying, "They [Chesapeake College] bring the courses to us, making them accessible to students. Over 50 percent of my seniors have taken a course at one time or another during high school."

Rhode Island

It appears that the only program available at the time of publication of this book is the Tech Prep Associate Degree Program which is articulated between the Community College of Rhode Island and participating high schools throughout the state. Most of the Tech Prep programs in the country allow students to receive some introductory course credits toward Associate of Applied Science Degrees or certificates from community colleges.

South Dakota

Guidelines for articulation of secondary school courses to technical institutes in South Dakota have been developed by the South Dakota Board of Education. Some of them are listed here:

1. To receive articulated credit, the student must have completed the high school course within the last three years;
2. A minimum of a "B" average in the course(s) to be articulated is required;
3. The credits articulated will count toward the total number needed for graduation from the program;
4. Transferable general education courses must meet CLEP, dual credit or Advanced Placement requirements (South Dakota Department of Education and Cultural Affairs, 1999).

California

In correspondence with Charles Klein, Specialist in Academic Planning in the Chancellor's Office of the California Community Colleges, it appears that California allows dual-credit programs under Education Code Section 66001. Community college course credit can be awarded to high school students if it is determined to be at a level appropriate by both the secondary school district and the community college district.

A pilot project was carried out between San Jose City College (SJCC) and San Jose Unified School District (SJUSD) in the spring semester of 1998. Both the governing boards of the high school and college districts approved the program. College-equivalent courses for high school students at various SJUSD sites allowed for the achievement of dual-credits. This was done under the title of CO-NECT. Ten courses were offered during the first semester in 1998. The courses had to be also available to the general public for enrollments.

While the California system Chancellor's Office has received a legal opinion showing that college credit can be granted for some high school courses and is not prohibited by law, it appears that many questions are still left unanswered. This appears to be a state moving toward clarification and support for clearer legislation and guidelines for dual-credit in the transfer or general education area.

Louisiana

The Louisiana Community and Technical College System (LCTCS) has some dual-credit arrangements but was unable to identify the level of action that is taking place in the state. Jerry Pinsel, from the LCTCS, in a letter to the author during the spring of 2001, indicated that Act 151 of the 1998 legislative session requires the Board of Regents to report activity regarding dual-credit/concurrent enrollment and/or articulation with secondary school students and community and technical colleges. He was in the process of collecting such data.

Delaware

Delaware Technical and Community College has articulation agreements with secondary school districts and awards up to ten college credits in specific technical programs and another six credits in academic core course departments. Agreements are in place in Biotechnology, Office Administration and Management Information Systems. More are being developed in the near future.

The National Alliance of Concurrent Enrollment Partnerships

A national group has been formed for professionals working with concurrent enrollment programs. *The National Alliance of Concurrent Enrollment Partnerships (NACEP)* now has its own website which also links a number of their member colleges. This alliance is designed to bring people together from colleges with high school programs offering college courses in high schools. In addition, it offers these other benefits:

NACEP supports and promotes its constituent programs through quality initiatives, program development, national standards, research, and communication (Website: "http://supa.syr.edu/nacep/" p.1).

This national alliance appears to be the only such group formed relative to dual-credit and/or concurrent enrollment programs. Their movement toward developing national standards, quality initiatives and research can only enhance and strengthen the dual-credit movement.

Some of the colleges that have joined the alliance include the following:

- Kenyon College in Ohio has offered college level courses on the high school campuses. The college assists by appointing faculty from the high schools to teach, evaluating the classes and course materials (jointly developed), and have cross-grading exercises between faculty of the high schools and the college.
- Indiana University, under its *Advance College Project*, has patterned its program after the Syracuse University's *Project Advance* program. Courses are offered in high schools throughout Indiana, Michigan and Ohio. The program was started in 1981 with one local Bloomington, Indiana, high school. The second year there were six high schools with 269 students enrolled. By 2000-2001 this program had grown to 90 high schools enrolling more than 1,500 secondary school students.
- A program entitled *The Cooperative Academic Partnership Program (CAPP)* is offered through the University of Wisconsin – Oshkosh. University approved high school instructors do the teaching. Approved classes are offered at the local Applied Technology Centers (ATC) and the Job Corps in the state. This university is one of the founding members of *The National Alliance of Concurrent Enrollment Partnerships*.
- The University of Missouri – Kansas City and the University of Missouri – St. Louis both have programs of advanced credit courses for high school students who have maintained a superior GPA and are recommended by faculty members.
- The University of Missouri-Kansas City program began in 1979 with five schools in two secondary school districts. It had grown by 1998-1999 to 619 classes in 55 high schools in 42 secondary school districts in the greater metropolitan Kansas City area. There were over 225 adjunct faculty involved in the program.

- The one community college listed as being linked to the national alliance network is Salt Lake Community College. Other community colleges are part of the alliance but were not yet linked to the NACEP web page.

It is at this point I want to point out that Concurrent Enrollment has been used to describe this national group and its movement. The teaching of the classes in the secondary schools would best appear to fit my definition of dual-credit.

Summary

While the titles vary from state-to-state, it is obvious that many states have formalized laws, policies and procedures to handle this new area of dual-credit and concurrent enrollment growth. Most of the programs listed above have evolved with formal and clearly defined processes and procedures during the 1990s with the exception of the Syracuse University program started in 1979, the Minnesota program started in 1985, and Vincennes University's program started in 1976. A number of states have recently started formalizing dual-credit programs. Some other states, while still early in the process of emerging with dual-credit or dual enrollment programs, have individual colleges and secondary schools working together in some isolated areas of their states.

The following two chapters are intended to differentiate dual-credit and concurrent enrollment programs that are developed as (1) those being offered *only* at a college campus and (2) those programs offered at *both* the college campus and at secondary schools.

Since dual-credit and concurrent enrollment programs are dynamic, changing quickly in their development, the division of programs offered may not remain up-to-date. They are, however, descriptive of how the programs were developed and should give the reader an excellent overview of the national picture of what has been developing in the arena of dual-credit programs for secondary school students.

The Dual-Credit Phenomenon!

III.

In 1986, the education establishment tried to gut the program. But the cat was out of the bag. When its supporters organized hearings, parents swarmed the capitol; they would not let it happen. Student after student showed up to say, "This transformed my life; I was bored; I didn't care about school; I wasn't even going to go to college, and this just made me come alive." (Minnesota's Post-Secondary Options Program: Odsborne & Gaebler)

State Plans: *College Campus and High School Campus Options*

There are 'state plans' for dual-credit or concurrent enrollment programs that utilize *both* the college campuses and high school campuses for the teaching of the courses. These plans offer flexibility to the secondary school students as to what courses are available and where they can be taken. Dual-credit course options are brought to local high schools in a number of states. In addition, students have the option of enrolling in both transfer and technical/vocational courses on the college campuses.

Courses taught at the secondary schools by high school teachers cause some concern in a few states. Some of these states have responded with clearly stated policies relative to the requirements necessary for faculty qualifications. In most states the requirements for secondary school faculty, or other adjunct faculty, to teach for the colleges are now the same as for full-time faculty on the campuses.

Other quality issues have centered on utilizing college textbooks, using the college course syllabuses, providing similar testing and writing requirements, and providing program and course review and supervision by faculty and administrators from the colleges. These patterns will emerge in the following state plans:

Alabama

The Alabama State Board of Education became the sole governing authority of the two-year college system in Alabama in 1998. In a 1997-98 *Chancellor's Special Report* the foundation was laid for expanding partnerships with secondary schools in the state. The report became approved policy of the Alabama State Board of Education and was entitled: *Admission: Dual Enrollment/Dual Credit for High School Students.*

The Alabama policy makes it clear that college classes offered for dual-credit may be taken at either the college campus *or* the high school. It is also clearly stated that students will receive *both* high school and college credit for these courses. There were eleven (11) Alabama colleges engaged in the program the first year (1997-98) and the prognosis was for more growth and expanded opportunities in subsequent years.

The monitoring of this program is to be carried out by the State Board of Education, the Chancellor of The Alabama College System, the State Superintendent of Schools, and the Executive Director of the Alabama Commission on Higher Education. Data collection, on-site visitation, program assessment, and annual evaluation plans are all included as part of the quality assurance of the Alabama program.

Arizona

The *State Board of Directors for Community Colleges of Arizona* under rule *R7-1-709: Community College Classes Offered in Conjunction with High Schools* establishes the requirements for offering community college courses in conjunction with high schools:

1. Students shall have been admitted to the community college in conjunction with provisions of 7-1-301 – Student Admissions and shall satisfy the prerequisites for the course as published in the college catalog.
2. Courses may be offered at the high school campus provided the courses have been evaluated and approved through the official college curriculum approval process.
3. Courses shall use college-approved textbooks, syllabuses, course outlines, and grading standards, all of which are applicable to the courses when taught at the community college campus.
4. Each faculty member shall have a valid community college teaching certificate in the field being taught and shall have been selected and evaluated by the college using the same procedure and criteria that are used at the community college campus.

Dr. Donald Puyear, Executive Director of the State Board of Directors for Community Colleges of Arizona reported that a study committee had been appointed by the legislature to look into questions regarding dual enrollment courses.

Idaho

Under their *Postsecondary Enrollment Options* program Idaho hopes to promote rigorous academic pursuits for secondary school students by allowing them to enroll either full- or part-time in postsecondary institutions. The institutions have to be "eligible institutions" which have been defined as:

Idaho public postsecondary institution; a private two-year trade and technical school accredited by a reputable accrediting association; or a private, residential, two-year or four-year liberal arts, degree granting college or university located in Idaho.

The Idaho State Board of Education sees this program as fostering its interest in accelerating learning programs for those qualified secondary students in the state. It identifies the programs as having the potential for reducing cost of secondary and postsecondary programs for both the students and the institutions.

It is expected that potential students in this program will be advised, as will their parents, about risks and possible consequences they might face by enrolling in postsecondary institutions. The student and his/her parents or guardian sign a form that is provided by the school district . This form confirms that they have received proper information and understand the responsibilities involved in enrolling in this program.

The statutes allow a student who enrolls at the secondary school less than four (4) hours a day to still be counted by the local school district for four (4) hours a day for purposes of state payment to the school. In addition, students who have been enrolled in these postsecondary programs are given priority when it is time to enroll in a postsecondary institution following secondary school graduation. The college credits earned in courses during the time of secondary school enrollment shall be included and/or accepted by the college when the student enrolls.

Students are charged the standard part-time credit hour fee or tuition, including activity fees, if the course is taken at the postsecondary institution campus.

Courses can be delivered at high schools and the costs are then borne by the post-secondary institution. The post-secondary institution charges the part-time credit hour fee or tuition, minus the on-campus activity fees. The three ways suggested in delivering courses to secondary schools are:

- through technology into the high school; or
- course(s) taught in the high school by post-secondary institution faculty; or
- a post-secondary institution employs high school faculty to teach the course(s).

Illinois

Illinois has developed a variety of program options for dual-credit students. There is no state legislation addressing this program. The Illinois Community College Board (ICCB) did much to increase the number of community colleges and secondary schools participating in the offering of dual-credit courses when it made a program change in 1997. The ICCB made a rule change to allow the colleges involved in dual-credit to obtain credit hour grants at the same time the secondary schools were able to obtain their average daily attendance funding from the state.

A major increase in program participation was attributed to the change in community college funding (Andrews, 2000). A 240% increase in the number of secondary schools participating was documented in a statewide study of the 48 community colleges in Illinois. The number increased from 120 to 290 secondary schools in the program between 1997-98 and 1999-2000.

Tuition is waived in the majority of the 48 Illinois community colleges for high school students enrolling in dual-credit. During fiscal year 2001 the ICCB was successful in obtaining a grant of one million dollars from the state legislature to use as "replacement tuition" for the tuition waivers being made. This grant money, while not fully covering the total amount of tuition waived, provided a very positive step in that direction.

The Illinois secondary school students enroll on the college campus, enroll in courses brought to the secondary schools, and are taught by both college teachers and qualified secondary school faculty. The programs adopt the college syllabuses and textbooks and properly pretest students who will enroll in English and mathematics classes.

Iowa

A *Postsecondary Enrollment Options Act* promotes rigorous academic and/or vocational and technical options for secondary school students who are identified as "gifted" in grades nine, ten, eleven and twelve. The Iowa Code allows enrollment part-time in nonsectarian courses in eligible postsecondary institutions of higher learning in Iowa:

> **Definition of an Eligible Postsecondary Institution**: An institution of higher learning under the control of the state board of regents, a community college, or an accredited private institution .

The Iowa act expects that the courses offered must not be ones that are already offered by the school districts or accredited nonpublic schools in which students are enrolled. The act also requires the secondary school districts to pay the tuition reimbursement to the postsecondary institutions in which their students enroll for classes. This program allows the students to attend courses at the postsecondary institutions or in their high school.

Kentucky

"Discover College," a program model in Kentucky at Owensboro Community College, is one of the many programs that will "increase Kentucky dual-credit programs dramatically," according to Dr. Keith Bird. Dr. Bird is Chancellor of Kentucky's Technical Colleges. Students can be admitted to dual-credit programs if they are recommended by a high school subject area teacher or other appropriate school official; have senior status; have a 60th percentile (national) ACT score in the subject area; and have a 3.25 high school grade point average.

Kentucky allows a maximum of four dual-credit courses for students. No more than two can be in any one discipline.

Minnesota

Minnesota developed their *Post-Secondary Enrollment Options Act in 1985*. High achieving secondary school students were then able to take college courses (Gerber, 1987).

Between 1985-86 and 1994-95 the program recorded growth from 3,528 students (3 percent of all eligible juniors and seniors) to 6,671 students representing 6 percent of the eligible pool of students. Approximately 45 percent of the students in 1994-95 were found to take courses at community colleges and 18 percent took classes through technical colleges (Minnesota Office of the Legislative Auditor, 1996).

Eligible institutions in Minnesota include public post-secondary Minnesota institutions. They also include private, nonprofit two-year trade and technical schools granting associate degrees, opportunities in industrialization centers accredited by the North Central Association of Colleges and Schools, or private, residential, two-year or four-year, liberal arts, degree-granting colleges or universities located in the state.

Pupils who start this program in grade 11 may petition for a maximum of two academic years of post-secondary courses to be used for secondary credit. If the student starts enrollment in the program in grade 12, the number of post-secondary courses to be utilized for secondary credit cannot be more than the equivalent of one academic year.

The courses can be taught by a secondary school teacher or a postsecondary faculty member, taught at secondary schools or at other locations as agreed upon by the secondary school and the postsecondary institution.

Credit can be used for either secondary credit or postsecondary school credit. Some credits are identified as secondary school credit and others as postsecondary credit.

Credits taken from a postsecondary institution that is listed on the students secondary school transcript will be marked as having been taken at a postsecondary institution and show the credits earned. The postsecondary school must award the credit so marked if the student decides to attend a postsecondary educational institution after secondary school graduation.

Missouri

In 1990 Missouri's General Assembly passed their first legislation allowing for high school students to be enrolled in college credit classes while in high school. State-aid was paid to secondary schools for the time students spent in the college courses. This greatly increased participation in the dual-credit program.

Quality control became a major issue in this program. The Missouri Coordinating Board of Higher Education (CBHE) conducted a survey of programs within the state in 1996. They found that a number of institutions had low standards due to a lack of quality controls.

The study was repeated in 1997-98 and found 34 Missouri institutions offering dual-credit in high schools to approximately 41,000 students (duplicated headcount). This was a 64% increase in the number reported two years previously. Both four-year and two-year colleges were involved. Problems still existed. Some postsecondary institutions did not accept the dual-credit courses. One of Missouri's most prominent institutions was among them.

The state set its focus on the quality of the program as it wanted to assure students that they could transfer the dual-credits earned. The CBHE adopted new guidelines starting in 1999. The goal of transferring of credit could now be assured for the students receiving dual-credit for courses from those postsecondary institutions in compliance with the policy. The students can now transfer up to five dual-credit courses. The *Coordinating Board for Higher Education* compiles and disseminates a list of policy-compliant institutions in the state. This is considered the "Good Housekeeping Seal of Approval" in the policy.

Nebraska

Information received from Sonia Cowen and Kathleen Fimple of the *Nebraska Coordinating Commission for Postsecondary Education* in Lincoln, Nebraska, indicated that Nebraska has no statutes supporting or detracting from dual-credit offerings. Efforts had been made over a seven or eight year period to implement a statewide agreement for dual-credit. Such an effort would provide uniform information for students and let them clearly know what credits would transfer to specific state institutions of higher education within the state.

A number of community colleges are offering dual-credit programs for juniors and seniors at institutions and at their high schools. One of the colleges offers a special five-year program with a secondary school where students can remain enrolled in the high school for a fifth year and achieve graduation with the associate degree and high school diploma simultaneously.

High school teachers, hired to deliver college level courses, are to have the same qualifications as regular college faculty.

The *Comprehensive Plan* for education in Nebraska calls for the following cooperation efforts between higher education and K/12 districts and schools:

Higher education will collaborate with K/12 districts and schools to assure statewide access to advanced placement and college-level courses for academically prepared students to facilitate a successful transition to postsecondary education course work:

- Enhance students' access to existing and emerging postsecondary education/high school programs by permitting academically-prepared high school students who are "on track" for high school graduation to be eligible to receive dual high school and college credit for the college-level courses they complete satisfactorily while attending high school.
- Promote high school students' participation in college-preparation and college-level instruction through programs such as Tech-Prep, School-to-Careers, high school-college academic summer courses and camps, and other such programs (Coordinating Commission for Postsecondary Education, Nebraska, 2001).

This comprehensive plan is relatively new and it will take time to determine how it deals with dual-credit classes across the state.

Nevada

Katrina Meyer of the Nevada University and Community College System reported to this writer in 2001that several college credit courses were being delivered to Nevada secondary school students at their high schools. Students are also allowed to enroll in courses on campus. Nevada does not gather state data or have state policies on these offerings. Whether a college course counts toward secondary school graduation depends upon the individual secondary school.

The Community College of Southern Nevada (CCSN) reported having over 30 high schools in their district and having dual-credit arrangements with all of them. Marion Littlepage, Program Director for CCSN, reported over 300 students enrolled in dual-credit courses during 2000-2001.

The college also has a high school housed on the community college campus. The *only* high school courses taught at this high school are mathematics, English and government. All other high school requirements are met through the use of college classes for dual-credit. In 2001 two students graduated from the college high school with their Associate Degrees at high school graduation time. Enrollment in the high school on campus program is selective and students must apply for consideration.

In addition, the Community College of Southern Nevada has provided three technical centers on three of the high school campuses. This has expanded the physical opportunities for technical programs in the dual-credit program.

New Jersey

New Jersey passed *The Higher Education Restructuring Act* in 1996, which allowed for accelerated student learning before and during college. The act calls for making better use of time and reducing the cost of college. With these new challenges, the state requires all colleges to make an annual report to the Commission of Higher Education on their course offerings in state high schools.

Syracuse University's *Project Advance,* from the state of New York, has been in existence since 1979 and is licensed to offer courses at New Jersey high schools. Courses have been offered in writing, English and textual studies, sociology, calculus and public affairs. Five high schools were involved in 1997.

Twenty-eight (56%) of the 50 New Jersey campuses reported having one or more college credit courses in New Jersey high schools during the five years prior to 1997. All three of the state's public universities and 16 out of the 19 community colleges reported offering courses in high schools.

Camden County College reported 34 courses through dual-credit arrangements during a five-year period starting in 1992. Courses were offered to 23 public and private secondary schools and included foreign languages, history, mathematics, sciences, accounting, principles of marketing, PASCAL, and FORTRAN.

Some dual-credit courses are taught by high school teachers who have the proper qualifications for teaching status at the community college or at the senior college or university. The majority of the faculty used to teach the high school courses are adjunct faculty with Master's Degrees or higher and five years of successful teaching experience.

There is no state title to identify the New Jersey dual-credit programs. Colleges within the state come up with their own formal names. Some of them are as follows: *Fast Start; Challenger Program; Credit Bank; High School Special Admissions Program; Program for Accelerated College Education; Credits-in-Escrow; Bridge Program; College Credit Bank for High Schools Students; High School Enrichment; Gifted and Talented;* and *Project Acceleration.*

The summary of the survey found 170 high schools being serviced through these programs. Sixty-three percent of the colleges reported an increase in the demand for this program was expected in the upcoming years (New Jersey Commission on Higher Education, 1997).

New York

The Syracuse University Project Advance (SUPA) is one of the best known and longest running concurrent enrollment programs in the country. It started in 1972 with seven local high schools wanting advanced work at the college level for their top students during the senior year.

This program has grown to serve five states. They are New York, New Jersey, Massachusetts, Maine and Michigan. There are approximately 3,800 students in the program from 120 high school districts (the website in September of 2001 was http://supa.syr.edu/SupaOnline/General/FactSheet.htm).

This writer was unable to obtain any other information relating to dual-credit programs in the state.

North Dakota

The North Dakota University System (NDUS) authorizes the offering of dual-credit courses and allows credit for both high school and college. The program received reaffirmation in 1997 by the Legislative Assembly in Senate Bill 2003. The program is open to juniors and seniors who have permission from secondary school administrators.

No limits were imposed in the legislation as to the number of credits or courses a student may enroll in for dual-credit. Dual-credit students pay the tuition costs. Information this writer received, however, indicated that tuition and fees students pay may change through legislative and State Board of Higher Education actions.

The courses must meet both content and academic standards of the same courses taught on the campuses. The college course syllabus and textbooks are utilized. These dual-credit courses are described as follows:

> The dual-credit courses taught in the high school are college courses which offers high school credit and *not* high school courses which receives college credit.

Most of the courses offered are the general education classes of the college. There are no special designations on the high school transcript to describe the course(s) as "dual-credit." In addition, each of these courses have equal transferability status within the North Dakota higher education system.

Instructors who are adjunct instructors for the colleges are approved through the same criteria as would be utilized for faculty employed on the campus. Preference is for Master Degrees in the subject field. If a college professor delivers the course in the high school it can be offered by the professor in person or via the distant learning network if such a link exists. North Dakota has determined that college faculty may teach these dual-credit courses in the high schools *without* having state secondary school certification.

Oklahoma

The *Oklahoma State Regents for Higher Education* (2000) summarized that there were 2,494 students enrolled in concurrent classes during 1998-99. This was an increase of 247 students from the previous year. Students can enroll at either the college campuses or in their local high schools. They may, however, enroll only in liberal arts and sciences courses if they enroll in off-campus courses or in electronic media courses. This limitation is not in effect for those students enrolling in on-campus classes.

Oklahoma offers students four (4) options, or environments, for the concurrent enrollment classes:

1. High school students enrolled on a college or university campus in a course with collegiate students enrolled;
2. High school students enrolled at an off-campus site in a course that originates on campus with collegiate students enrolled;
3. High school students enrolled in a course with collegiate students enrolled at an established off-campus site with a regular program of study (defined as Associate of Arts, Associate of Science, or Baccalaureate degree);
4. High school students enrolled at other off-campus sites (including in-the-home and including the use of synchronous or asynchronous instruction) and taught by *regular faculty* (emphasis added) whose primary employment is as a faculty member at the institution delivering the course. Exceptions may be considered on a case-by-case basis.

Regular faculty was defined as persons qualified for appointment to the regular faculty of the college proposing to award credit. This faculty definition appears to have the intent of limiting the colleges from hiring secondary school teachers to teach the college classes as concurrent or dual-credit classes. The language, "primary employment as a faculty member at the institution delivering the course," appears limiting in nature.

South Carolina

Fifteen of the sixteen South Carolina technical colleges were offering dual-credit coursework in local high schools according to information received by this writer in late 1999. The South Carolina Technical College utilized a State Board procedure for the articulation of this coursework from secondary to postsecondary schools. Included in this articulation procedure are the following recommendations:

1. Delineation of the courses and/or programs to be offered as part of the articulation agreement;
2. The number of secondary credits and postsecondary advanced placement credits to be awarded, if applicable;
3. If applicable, the levels of performance or standards to be maintained by students in order for postsecondary credits to be awarded;
4. The procedures and requirements pertaining to the enrollment of secondary students in the articulated program.

Tennessee

Junior and senior level high school students may enter college courses for both high school and college credit or dual enrollment as defined in Tennessee. Both universities and community colleges are involved in the program.

The admission policies are from the Tennessee Board of Regents system (TBR) and students are enrolled as non-degree admission status. Fall semester of 2000 found 75 students enrolled in TBR universities and a total of 2,822 in two-year institutions.

Faculty may be hired from the college or from the secondary school teaching staffs to deliver instruction. Courses are delivered in high schools or on college campuses. Standard qualifications are required for teachers. This information was provided by Kay Clark, Associate Vice Chancellor for Academic Affairs, Tennessee Board of Regents.

Texas

The Texas *Coordinating Board for Texas Higher Education,* in 1998, encouraged dual-credit programs by making several rule amendments affecting public two-year associate degree-granting institutions.

> The Coordinating Board encourages and supports partnerships between secondary schools and public two-year Associate-degree granting institutions, including such initiatives as Tech-Prep and concurrent course credit which allow secondary students to receive both high school and college-level credit for college-level courses.

These partnerships needed to include (1) student eligibility requirements; (2) faculty qualifications; (3) location and student composition of classes; (4) provision of student learning and support services; (5) eligible courses; (6) grading criteria; (7) transcribing of credit; and (8) funding provisions.

Students must pass the Texas Academic Skills Program (TASP) test or a Board-approved alternative assessment in a minimum of one area such as mathematics, reading or writing. The test must be deemed applicable by the college in which the student will be enrolling for the concurrent course(s). Students are limited to two college credit courses per semester unless there are special circumstances. Exceptions are made for exceptional academic abilities based upon grade-point average, ACT or SAT scores, or other assessment indicators.

Faculty must meet minimal requirements as outlined by the Commission on Colleges of the Southern Association of Colleges and Schools. The faculty members are expected to meet the same standards, review, and approval procedures that are utilized by the college as it selects faculty for the same courses taught on the main campus of the college.

Courses can be taught at the secondary school or the main campus of the college. It is, however, specified that these concurrent credit courses taught at the secondary school should be composed of only concurrent, advanced placement (AP), and/or college credit students. Some exceptions might be made and one of them is that the mixed class is limited to enrollment of high school honors students, all of whom will be taught the college-level course.

Courses that apply to this partnership agreement are:

> College-level academic courses listed in the current edition of the Community College General Academic Course Guide Manual or as college-level technical courses in an approved Tech-Prep or Associate of Applied Science (AAS) degree or certificate program.

The level of instruction as well as the materials for a course must be at the equivalent level for the identical course taught on the main campus of the colleges.

Funding is available to both public school districts and public two-year associate degree-granting institutions. Tuition and fee waivers are granted for some of the colleges to award to students. The public community/junior college may waive the tuition and fees if a Texas public high school student enrolls in college courses giving concurrent course enrollment credits. The rules also state that public technical colleges and other public two-year associate degree-granting institutions may not waive the tuition and fees. This wording is confusing and the last two statements seem to be in conflict with each other.

Utah

Salt Lake Community College (SLCC) offers a concurrent enrollment program for both high school and college credit. The instructors are high school faculty who qualify as adjunct faculty for SLCC. In their promotional materials the college identifies instructor qualifications, syllabi, assignments, textbooks, exams and grading requirements as being equivalent to the same courses on the campus.

Seniors, and some qualified juniors, may enroll in the SLCC program. It is the high school that identifies the qualified students. Students may select from both general education and vocational offerings. The individual schools decide what courses they would like the college to offer.

Virginia

The state of Virginia offers dual-enrollment courses at the high schools or on the community college campuses. The classes can meet secondary school course requirements or be used as electives. The secondary schools pay for the tuition and students pay for their books. Both the secondary school and community college systems are funded for these courses.

Some of the four-year colleges also offer high school students the concurrent enrollment opportunity. Most of the offerings are on the college campus. Some may be utilized for dual-credit purposes.

The state of Virginia promotes the need for *equivalency* in their dual-credit program:

> Equivalency is necessary if students who transfer to four-year institutions are to receive credit for dual-credit instruction, thus enabling them to complete baccalaureate degrees without taking additional credits (Carr, p. 1).

Equivalency is addressed by having (1) course equivalencies, (2) student readiness and eligibility, (3) student placement, (4) faculty qualifications and evaluation, (5) faculty orientation and development and (6) student outcome assessment.

Faculty members who teach in the dual-credit program are to have the same qualifications as the persons teaching the same courses on the campuses. They must meet both Virginia Community College System requirements as well as those of the Southern Association of Colleges and Schools.

Each college has the responsibility to assure students are receiving the same level of quality instruction in the dual-credit program as students on campus or in other off-campus sites of the college.

Wisconsin

The State of Wisconsin, Department of Public Instruction, updated its dual-enrollment program and it is now included in the

Wisconsin's Youth Options Program (1998). This replaced the *Postsecondary Enrollment Options* program that had been in existence since 1992-93.

The new regulations makes it clear that a student can now earn a high school diploma whether the requirements are met through attendance at a college or while attending the high school. The new program expands the opportunities to students wishing to pursue a technical career program, attend college early, or prepare to enter the workforce following high school graduation.

Classes can now be taken at a University of Wisconsin institution (there are several throughout Wisconsin), one of the Wisconsin technical colleges, or one of the private nonprofit institutions in the state. All of the University of Wisconsin System institutions and all campuses of the Wisconsin Technical College System colleges participate. The private, nonprofit institutions and the Wisconsin tribally controlled colleges have the option to participate on a year-to-year basis. During the 2000-2001 school year all of these institutions elected to participate.

Credit can be counted toward college as well as high school graduation once it has been properly approved for a student. The basic intent of this program is to allow students to access postsecondary courses not available in their high schools.

All of the public high schools in Wisconsin are required to participate. Parents must provide for the transportation between the secondary school and the college program.

Information received from the Wisconsin Technical College System has recorded Youth Option student enrollments of 1,542 in fiscal year 1999, 2,037 in fiscal year 2000, and 2,147 in fiscal year 2001.

Technical college courses may be delivered at the technical college, the high school or through one of the alternate methods of delivery (e.g., distance education, internet, or ITV). Articulation agreements with high schools allow for Tech Prep credits to be part of the dual-credits that transfer with him/her to the technical college at time of enrollment after high school.

Wyoming

The Wyoming Community College Commission has had a concurrent enrollment program since 1995. It is the *Wyoming Postsecondary Education Options Program.* In 1997 a survey of concurrent enrollment practices was undertaken statewide.

All seven of the community colleges and the University of Wyoming accept student credits earned in this program. The community colleges are all involved in offering courses in the program and the University of Wyoming had been in the process of negotiating with a local high school for a program when this information was received.

Faculty travel from the community colleges to the high schools. High school students attend and take classes on the campuses and can attend classes at the high school taught by high school teachers who qualify as adjunct faculty. The course syllabuses and textbooks from the college are used for these courses.

Both high school juniors and seniors may enroll. They must have better than average grade point averages, have high school principal recommendations, and pass diagnostic placement tests in some courses and also meet course prerequisites. In the state survey it was not unusual to find students in the program had accomplished 12 to 15 credit hours of college work before graduating from high school.

Funding for some of the high schools and their students in this program came from Boards of Cooperative Education Services (BOCES). Some colleges received payment from school districts to cover tuition and fees. Some colleges received funds directly from the BOCES in their district. Payments differed throughout the state and came from a variety of sources including the students. The most frequent payment process was identified as the colleges billing the high schools for tuition and fees and paying the high schools for their faculty teaching college classes.

Summary

The above states have developed comprehensive dual-credit programs for secondary school students. This chapter has reviewed the states that allow students the option of attending dual-credit classes on the campus of the college or at the local high school.

Faculty selected for these programs are usually selected through the hiring guidelines in each community college state plan. In addition, the regional accrediting association guidelines are being utilized to assure quality faculty are provided for dual-credit classes whether they are on the campus or in the local high school.

IV.

Dual-credit courses achieve multiple purposes. The primary purpose of offering dual-credit courses is to deliver high-quality college experiences to high-performing high school students. Dual-credit courses also enrich and extend the high school curriculum, provide introductory coursework, and avoid unnecessary duplication in coursework as students move from high school to college (Missouri Coordinating Board for High Education, 1999).

State Plans: *College Campus Programs*

A number of states have developed dual-credit and/or concurrent enrollment programs that may *only be taken* on a college campus. Students are expected to drive to the campus and take courses with other students on the campus. States in which this is the only option are Alaska, Arkansas, Connecticut, Hawaii, Kansas, Massachusetts, Michigan, Mississippi, Montana, and New Mexico.

Alaska

The University of Alaska-Anchorage promotes its Credit-by-Choice Program for high school students wishing to obtain dual-credit. The university suggests students take general education courses and move more quickly through their education:

> Taking classes at the university while in high school, even just one per semester and two in summers during your junior and senior years, give you enough university credits to nearly complete your freshman year before you graduate from high school (University of Alaska, 2000, p.1).

Arkansas

The law in Arkansas encourages early enrollment options for secondary school students to enroll in college-level courses. The credit earned can be used for both college credit and high school diploma completion.

In 1999 Senate Concurrent Resolution 20 was passed. The Resolution required the Arkansas Higher Education Coordinating Board to work with the State Board of Education and the State Board of Workforce Education and Career Opportunities to address eight (8) areas of common concern relative to concurrent enrollment programs.

The definitions used in Arkansas are opposite of those used by this author. In Arkansas dual enrollment is considered for college-level credit only. Concurrent enrollment allows for high school credit and college-level credit. The students enroll in college campus courses.

The colleges and universities are allowed to obtain college state funding for semester credit hours if (1) the institution awards college credit in either vocational or non-vocational course offerings; and (2) the institution receives tuition paid by the student, a scholarship, an independent fund, or by the high school district.

Testing of students planning to enroll in college English and mathematics courses is required. The faculty selected to teach the concurrent courses must hold the same credentials as other adjunct faculty at the institution.

Connecticut

The Connecticut Community Colleges have a long-standing Board Policy on dual-credit for high school students. The rules utilized were adopted on June of 1987 and have been amended.

The dual-credit opportunities are viewed as providing especially talented high school students with more challenging educational experiences than may be available in high school. They also provide options for capable students who appear to be "turned off" by high school. These students, by enrolling in one or two college

---

classes a semester, may find themselves motivated to complete high school rather than drop out.

Admission of high school age students under the Connecticut high school partnerships program utilizes the following guidelines:

1. Each community-technical college, acting through the president, may enter into written agreements with (a) the superintendents of schools of area school districts, (b) the directors of state regional vocational-technical high schools, and (c) the administrative heads of parochial high schools for the admission of high school students to community-technical college.
2. Juniors and seniors with a minimum of eighty percent scholastic average will be eligible for admission.
3. The school district may offer concurrent or supplemental high school credit for courses taken at a community-technical college in accord with program guidelines.
4. High school students admitted to the program will be eligible to enroll in a maximum of two community-technical college credit courses each semester. In the case of high school seniors in their last term, the two-course limit may be exceeded on the recommendation of the school principal.
5. The college will pay the costs of tuition for the high school students participating in the program and will waive all fees.
6. The school district and/or the participating students will be responsible for the cost of books and transportation. The school district will be encouraged to purchase books to loan or give to participating students.*

*Connecticut data provided by Karen Sue Grosz, Chief Academic Officer, Connecticut Community College System, Hartford, CT. (2001).

Hawaii

A newly created *Running Start (RS)* program was announced in Hawaii during 2001. The first semester of the program involved six (6) Honolulu District high schools. The eight classes available in the program drew nineteen (19) students during spring semester of 2001 and fifteen (15) were expected for the summer of 2001.

The University of Hawaii Community College system and the

State of Hawaii Department of Education will attempt to expand this program considerably in the future. Discussions were underway at the publication time of this book. Material on Hawaii was furnished by Jean Maslowski of the Hawaii Community College (HCC) system. (2001).

Kansas

The *Kansas Challenge to Secondary School Pupils Act* challenges school districts to cooperate with postsecondary school institutions and provide new and exciting challenges to secondary school pupils. It encourages them to take advantage of the wealth of postsecondary school options available in Kansas. Kansas defines a concurrent enrolled student as follows:

> **Definition**: "Concurrent enrollment pupil" means a person who is enrolled in either of the grades 11 or 12 within a school district, has demonstrated the ability to benefit from participation in the regular curricula of eligible postsecondary education institutions, has been authorized by the principal of the school attended to apply for enrollment at an eligible postsecondary institution, and is acceptable or has been accepted for enrollment at an eligible postsecondary education institution.

The Act recognizes that the credit may be achieved for college credit and at the same time for dual-credit status for both college and secondary school. The college credit is to count toward a degree or certificate of the college.

Kansas requires the student to pay the institution the negotiated amount of tuition that is charged by the postsecondary institution in which the student enrolls. The student is also responsible for books and other fees of enrollment.

Massachusetts

As a part of the state *Education Reform Act* of 1993 the Commonwealth of Massachusetts establish *The Dual Enrollment Program*. This is a program which allows students to gain both college credit and high school credit work simultaneously. Thirty Massachusetts public colleges and universities participate.

The enrollment in this program was over 1,200 students during the spring of 1999. Between 1993 and the 1999 report there were over 9,000 students in the state who had benefited from this new program. Students have to meet the pertinent requirements of the college or university in which they enroll and generally have a 3.00 grade point average as a minimum.

The Massachusetts Department of Education provides the public institutions of higher education a tuition reimbursement for costs per credit hour. In 1999-2000 the reimbursement for credit hour payments were established as follows: (1) University of Massachusetts $150; (2) State colleges $100; (3) Community colleges $70.

Participants may select either academic or occupational college-level courses if the occupational courses are not available at the local high schools of the students. The public high school, at its discretion, may treat the college level courses as *honor* level classes and, therefore, give the student one grade higher on the high school transcript than that earned for the college credit.

The dual-credit classes must be offered *at* the colleges and qualify as dual-credit for the students. Courses *cannot* be brought to the secondary schools, nor be offered through distance learning courses or through technology (internet), or correspondence if they are to count as dual-credit.

Michigan

Michigan has a dual-enrollment program. It falls under the *Postsecondary Enrollment Options Act Update* started in the fall of 1999. The program was originally started in 1991 as a means to keep high school students continually challenged and interested in their academic pursuits. Those students who have taken all of the MEAP High School Test areas and received endorsement in the subject area they wish to have for dual-enrollment credit may be enrolled. Students may also enroll in college classes where there are no endorsement areas on the MEAP Test. These areas are in such courses as philosophy, religion, psychology, sociology, anthropology, computer science and/or foreign languages.

Students may elect to take courses during their regular school day, evenings, weekends, on- or off-campus, or by interactive television. They have the option of utilizing courses for high school credit, college credit, or for both purposes. This program appears to be a dual-credit program option as defined in this book.

The secondary school district generally provides all tuition and fee payments for the students enrolled in the college courses. Schoolcraft College in Southeastern Michigan requires that students have to take required testing prior to enrolling in English, mathematics or in reading. It does not charge the dual-credit students for this service.

Mississippi

Under the Junior College sections of Mississippi law (Junior Colleges, Chapter 29, 2000) the boards of trustees of the community and junior colleges are authorized to establish dual-credit programs. Students are required to meet the requirements to enroll in a community college while they are still enrolled in high school. These include:

(a) Students must have completed a minimum of fourteen (14) core high school units;

(b) Students must have a minimum ACT composite score of twenty-one (21) or the equivalent SAT score;

(c) Students must have a 3.0 grade point average on a 4.0 scale, or better, on all high school courses, as documented by an official high school transcript (home schooled students must submit a transcript prepared by parent, legal guardian or custodian's written recommendation);

(d) Students must have an unconditional written recommendation from their high school principal and/or guidance counselor. Home schooled students must submit a parent, legal guardian or custodian's written recommendation.

Students can continue to be counted for average daily attendance at the public school they attend.

Montana

During the 2001 Montana legislative session House Bill No. 265 was introduced allowing 11th and 12th grade students to attend *colleges of technology*. The bill allows for the classes to be tuition-free and allows students to enroll in those classes that are not available through the students' local school district. It is called the *Running Start Program* and allows students to earn both high school and college credits. The bill states that the student is responsible for his/her own transportation, books and supplies. The Superintendent of Public Instruction for the state of Montana is to be given the authority to develop a means of administering the agreements necessary between the high school districts and the colleges of technology.

In April of 2001 the Governor signed into law HB 265. The final version of the bill opens the enrollment for secondary school 11th and 12th students to the Montana university system, a public community college, or a tribal college. The final version appears much more comprehensive in terms of course selection for students.

New Jersey

Drew University in New Jersey is a private university offering outstanding juniors and seniors the opportunity to enroll in their *High School Enrichment Program*. Some of the general education offerings are in mathematics, classics, psychology, English literature and history.

The cost per course was $1,458 during the 2000-2001 academic year. The credits may be applied to Drew University degrees or transferred to other colleges. Courses are only offered through enrollment at the university campus.

North Carolina

The *Huskins Bill* and the *State Board of Community Colleges* set the guidelines for concurrent enrollment programs in North

Carolina. Students may take college courses at a community college while enrolled in high school. The objectives for the program are:

(1) to provide a program for selected high school students to participate in college credit educational opportunities not other wise available;

(2) to enhance the motivation and achievement of high school students;

(3) to improve the equalization of opportunities among high schools throughout the state by offering college credit courses; and,

(4) to encourage high school students to utilize post secondary opportunities as a means for pursuing lifelong educational goals (*North Carolina Community College System* and the *North Carolina Department of Public Instruction*, p. 14-1).

High school students enrolling in these college credit courses are to be exempt from tuition. The boards of education are to be responsible for textbooks and fees (other than tuition) for their high school students enrolled in community colleges. The Huskins Bill includes the following language:

> *...Local administrative boards and local school boards may establish cooperative programs in the areas they serve to provide for college courses to be offered to qualified high school students with college credits to be awarded to those high school students on successful completion of the courses...subject to the rules of the State Board of Community Colleges.*

Enrollment data provided from the North Carolina Community College System indicated that enrollments totaled 10,959 students for the 2000-2001 school year. These numbers compare with 3,031, 3,714, and 4,214 in academic years 1997-1998, 1998-1999, and 1999-2000, respectively.

North Dakota

North Dakota has vocational-technical programs that offer dual credit options with high school students. They are under the Tech

Prep umbrella. Black Hills State University offers dual enrollment options to students who (1) have a minimum of a 2.7 cumulative GPA and junior or senior status; (2) rank in the top half of their class; (3) have a written recommendation from their high school counselor or principal; (4) have permission of the instructor and (5) meet all course prerequisites.

Communications from Nouth Dakota brought out the fact that there have been some changes relative to academic dual-credit through the Board of Regents. Nothing was published at the time of this research.

West Virginia

The Southern West Virginia Community and Technical College has an early entry for high school students who are juniors or seniors. They are allowed to enroll if they have a 3.0 (B) or higher average and a consent form from the principal or counselor and a parent. The credit hours allowed can be a maximum of four a semester for juniors and a maximum of seven for seniors unless special permission is received from the Vice President of Academic Affairs.

Summary

The development of dual-credit and concurrent enrollment options in the above states has remained somewhat more conservative and limiting in opportunities than in those states allowing enrollment in both college campus and secondary school college credit offerings.

It is possible that some of the above states also allow students to enroll in dual-credit classes at the local high school. The laws, procedures, and other reports received by this author did not offer this option in any of their written materials. This is such a dynamic movement that the information could be outdated by the time of publication of this book.

There appears to be a number of reasons that students are limited to the campus programs in some states. One reason is that the questions on faculty qualifications do not become an issue. The proximity of colleges to the majority of secondary schools is another issue in some states. If students have the opportunity to get to a college campus within reasonable driving distance then the campus-only option may work.

Some states, and universities, are still dealing with the college campus environmental issue of whether the college course being offered at secondary schools is a viable option. Some believe that regular college students should be enrolled in the same course as the secondary school students in order to offer the student a college environment for learning. This reasoning breaks down considerably when one sees that Advanced Placement (AP) classes are accepted at full-credit while offered in secondary schools. Some universities also offer correspondence, internet and other forms of course delivery which do not provide any of the type of collegiate environment that is sometimes argued as being necessary relative to dual-credit classes.

These campus-only plans have, however, paved the way for thousands of secondary school students to get a head start on college level coursework.

V.

Any program which serves a large population in a diversity of settings needs to be regularly monitored and evaluated. The Community College System must ensure the rigor of dual enrollment courses by requiring individual colleges to adhere to the standards put forth in the Guidelines for Dual Enrollment Inter-institutional Articulation Agreements (Florida State Board of Community Colleges, 1997, p. 11).

Quality Issues: Lessons Learned from Missouri and Florida

The number one concern, as dual-credit programs have quickly expanded across states, has been guaranteeing students consistency in *quality* of instruction and transferability of coursework taken.

In this chapter the two states of Missouri and Florida are highlighted. Missouri started out strong in the dual-credit movement but ran into some serious concerns. Quality was challenged as well as the transferability of a number of the courses from the colleges offering dual-credit courses. In Florida a poorly conducted research report jolted the community colleges involved in dual-credit programming in the state. Two of the community colleges fought back and conducted their own research. The outcomes of this research helped the community colleges to regain the thrust necessary to continue and expand the dual-credit movement in Florida.

Lessons Learned: The Missouri Experience

In the state of Missouri, the Missouri Coordinating Board for Higher Education adopted new policy guidelines June 10, 1999. These new guidelines were to be fully implemented by the fall 2000 academic semester. The guidelines were entitled: *Policy Guidelines for the Delivery and Transferability of Credit Obtained in Dual Credit-Programs Offered in High School With Draft Clarifying Comments.*

Purposes

The two main *purposes* identified for the dual-credit program in Missouri in the new policy guidelines of 1999 are : (1) to deliver high-quality college experiences to high-performing high school students; and (2) to enrich and extend the high school curriculum, provide introductory college coursework, and avoid unnecessary duplication in coursework as students move from high school to college (p. 2).

The Need for New Guidelines

These new guidelines in Missouri came about as a result of several years of large growth and problems in dual-credit programs across the state. These programs had very mixed success and a *standard for quality* had not been established. Some of the universities refused to consider transferring credit from these programs.

The dual-credit program increased by 64% between the two years of 1995-1996 and 1997-1998. The duplicated headcount in the state stood at 41,000 students in 1997-1998. The majority of these enrollments were from the three largest programs in the state. They were primarily at four-year institutions. Community colleges began having a larger role in providing these numbers as well (Girardi and Stein, p. 15).

In 1996, the Missouri Coordinating Board conducted a survey of dual-credit programs. They found a number of significant deficiencies in the administration of these dual-credit programs:

(1) many dual-credit students had no access to college resources;
(2) instructors did not always use the same syllabi as used in the on-campus courses; and
(3) many instructors were lacking the qualifications recommended by the North Central Association and Missouri's regional accrediting body (p. 14).

Another survey in 1997-1998 documented continuing problems. They found some programs with the following deficiencies:

(1) various degrees of connectivity to on-campus programs;
(2) administration of programs by the departments of continuing education on the campus;
(3) courses where only *some* of the students took the course for the college credit (mixed classes);
(4) variation in student eligibility requirements,
(5) minimal teaching credentials by faculty teaching in the program; and
(6) "quality assurance practices" were variable throughout the state (p. 15).

Key Issues to Address

The threat of disrupting existing articulation agreements with universities in the state was disturbing. One key university in the state refused to accept any dual-credit classes from incoming students. Some of the universities and colleges in which the students had obtained their dual-credits were also refusing to accept their own dual-credit classes toward further degree work!

It became evident that the state needed a uniform policy that addressed these identified problems. The problems of program inputs needed to be addressed. These problems included student eligibility, faculty qualifications, program quality, program supervision by university faculty, and others (pp. 16-17).

New Missouri Guidelines, 1999

The new Missouri guidelines addressed transfer courses only. No attempt was made to deal with technically oriented classes that the colleges may offer. The key elements in these new guidelines were:

1. Dual-credit courses may be taught by full-time college faculty who instruct high school students either on campus or in the high school via on-site instruction or interactive television.
2. Dual-credit courses may also be taught, using the same modes of delivery, by adjunct faculty who may teach part-time both on the college campus and at the high school site.
3. The majority of dual credit courses are taught by high school faculty, with supervision by on-campus college faculty (p. 1).

Student Eligibility for Enrollment

It was decided to allow the admission standards of the college or university to determine eligibility of students in dual-credit classes. The policy guidelines, however, did specify that, "students must have a minimum overall grade-point average of 3.0 (on a 4.0 scale) or the equivalent, and be recommended by the high school principal or his or her official designee (p. 2)." In addition, students must meet the identical requirements to enroll in specific classes such as English and mathematics as is required for students enrolling as on-campus students. This refers to testing such as the ACT, ASSET, or individual college placement tests for these courses. Some high school freshmen or sophomores are allowed to enroll under special circumstances. The policy refers to having these students score a minimum of the 90th percentile on the ACT or SAT tests. A counselor must also concur that such students would be able to benefit and have the maturity to succeed.

Quality Checkpoints

The following are what this author will refer to as the *quality checkpoints* of the Missouri plan:

(1) Courses must duplicate the identical course offerings delivered on campus to students matriculated there;
(2) Credit must be deemed acceptable for transfer by the faculty of the appropriate academic department of the college;

(3) On-campus faculty must identify the syllabus, textbook(s), teaching methodology, and student assessment strategies;

(4) The chief academic office of the college is responsible for identifying the appropriate faculty on-campus to oversee the selection and evaluation of all dual-credit faculty;

(5) Students in these classes must have geographic access to student and academic support similar to that of on-campus students. Such support includes library resources and reasonable access to the course instructor outside of the classroom hours;

(6) Faculty must be qualified as determined by the requirements of the North Central Association of College and Schools and the Commission on Institution of Higher Education. This implies having a Master's Degree with a minimum of 18 hours in the subject field to be taught;

(7) Student assessment and evaluation measures, assuring quality, must be put in place similarly to those on campus;

(8) Annual reports must be prepared relative to student performance in order to determine continuation of specific faculty teaching in the program;

(9) Students are to be guaranteed that five of the dual-credit courses will be transferred to any college or university in Missouri. More may be taken by individual students with the guideline of having the student check with the college or university he/she may be considering transferring to after high school. This is to determine if more than five courses are taken in the program, the additional courses will also transfer (pp. 3-6).

The chief academic office on the college campus has the responsibility for these policy guidelines being met.

The state of Missouri and its development of state standards for dual-credit programs can be seen as an exceptional example for states across the country to consider. Many states are still developing programs at a fast pace with little guidance as to quality standards.

Lessons from The Florida Experience

Another set of lessons has come out of the experience of the community college system of Florida. The dual-credit system became threatened by limited and inaccurate research.

A major fear was struck in 1993 when the University of Florida published a report indicating that, "the vast majority of former dual enrollment (DE) students entering the institution had to retake these courses (Legg, 1993)." The report focused upon those students who had *not* met the regular State University System criteria for admissions. One can only imagine the anxiety and anger that was raised throughout the Florida community college system when this report was published.

Had the state financed a program of dual enrollments that had failed to the point that the state would now have to pay for students to repeat these courses? Would the program survive when secondary school administrators, parents and students learned of the findings in this report?

It wasn't long before two of the largest Florida community colleges took it upon themselves to conduct research of their own relative to the success of their former students who had transferred to universities in the state. Pensacola Junior College (PJC) and Tallahassee Community College (TCC) put their research focus upon those students who met the regular admissions requirements at these universities.

Both Pensacola Junior College and Tallahassee Community College focused upon those students in universities most often attended by their graduates. These were the University of West Florida (UWF) for PJC and the Florida State University (FSU) for TCC.

Pensacola Junior College looked at a cohort of students who took the first and second level of English transfer classes. This provided a sample of 68 students. Each student had successfully completed a dual-credit class in English during the 1991-1992 school year (Atwell, 1994, p.1).

There were two performance outcomes that the Pensacola people studied: (1) grade point average and (2) grades received in advanced writing classes at the University of Western Florida (UWF).

The results showed a grade point average (g.p.a.) of 2.82 for the fifty-two dual enrollment students who had enrolled at UWF. The State Board of Community Colleges (SBCC) showed in their report (1994) that this 2.82 g. p. a. was the same as for all Pensacola Junior College students at UWF. They also found that the four of the six students scoring less than a 2.00 g. p. a. had earned a "C" grade in one or both of the English dual enrollment classes. They also had low g. p. a.'s overall from the dual-enrollment program.

Only 13 PJC students were found to have taken advanced writing courses at UWF. It was determined that, even with a small number, the results were positive. There were eight in the A, B, or C range and two that were in the D/F range. The two students who received less than "C" grades were students in dual enrollment classes who had achieved C's in one or both of the dual enrollment English classes. They were, also, both low g. p. a. students previous to enrolling at UWF.

Tallahassee Community College identified 64% of the cohort group from both fall semesters of 1990 and 1991. This was a total of 191 and 196 individuals out of a possible 352 and 391 respectively.

Courses and Outcomes

Tallahassee Community College compared grade distributions at Florida State University for *dual enrollment* students and *regular students*. What they found was that the dual enrollment students did very well in this comparison:

> The initial comparison of grades earned by dual enrollment (DE) status students indicated that the grades earned by DE students were clearly higher than those earned by regular students in both sets of courses.

How would these same students compare when tracked individually in the next level course?

TCC next looked at English and Western Civilization to check progress. What they found was that the dual enrollment students did better in the second course than the regular students. TCC did not find this surprising since the DE students had previously had to pass a college placement test and be recommended by the high school principal before they could be enrolled in a DE class. In short, there were quality controls set in place during entry into the dual-enrollment classes.

State Survey Follow-up

The state of Florida community college system became interested in learning about the success of dual enrolled students across the state. A statewide survey was conducted by the Division of Community Colleges. This survey provided data on the success of dual enrollment students enrolled in the State University System (SUS).

The study included all dual enrolled students from the 1991-1992 year. There were 17,981 dual enrollment students included in this study. The main outcome of this study was, "the passing rate for dual enrollments was higher than that of entering community college freshmen (p. 8)."

Repeat Courses from Statewide Data

The study did much to shatter the study that had been published by a researcher at the University of Florida. The data on dual-credit students repeating courses showed the following:

1. In the 1991-1992 study there were 51,382 unique dual enrollments (an enrollment of a student in a given course);
2. These enrollments were matched against data from 1992-1995 and only 140 matches were found that indicated a former dual enrollment student had *retaken* a course at the university level;
3. This amounted to less than 1% of dual-credit students having to repeat a course.

Further investigation of the data on students repeating classes indicated 42 of these 140 students repeated English. Research found that less than half of these students had been successful in English when they were a dual enrollment student. In short, they had not earned a "C" grade or better the first time. This pattern did not differ from the regular students having to repeat a course.

The summary of this important research study was presented as follows:

> With thousands of students being served by twenty-eight different institutions, it is probably inevitable that not every student will be accelerated. However, based upon the results of these studies, there is no reason to believe the dual enrollment program, as currently implemented in the Florida Community College System, is not providing a viable acceleration mechanism for qualified high school students (p. 12).

This review of the Florida *research* on dual enrollment students has provided a valuable experience from which other states can learn. When the original study was released from the University of Florida, the dual enrollment program statewide could have been in jeopardy.

Summary

This chapter has looked at two different dual enrollment programs in the states of Missouri and Florida. The Missouri program started expanding at a pace that surpassed the development of standards that were needed to assure proper quality for transferring to the state college and university system.

Missouri made changes which established the credibility needed for these dual-credit programs as they relate to students, secondary schools, parents, and transferability to colleges and universities. Missouri weathered some extreme setbacks in the early years of growth in dual-credit programs. The state did, however, "bite the bullet" and address the major points of concern in order to assure quality in their program. Some may argue that it has taken away much of the freedom and local decision-making. In the meantime the program has a foundation for success in the immediate future if the guidelines are followed by each of the colleges.

Florida's dual enrollment program had a *scare* due to limited data of a negative nature being produced by a prominent university in Florida. Two large community colleges conducted research that completely reversed the results of the previously limited study of dual enrollment students.

Their follow-up research documented the fact that dual enrollment students were, indeed, successful. They were found to have greater success at universities than the *regular* enrolled students. A statewide follow-up study further documented this success. It would appear that when proper research is conducted on programs that have the quality inputs in place the results bear out the success of the dual-credit programs.

The two state case studies have documented the need to have quality inputs and quality comprehensive research regarding the success of persons in dual-credit programs. State community college systems can work to help ensure that dual-credit programs throughout a state can be monitored to assure they adhere to the standards necessary to ensure students *transfer of credits* as well as to provide *credibility* of the dual-credit program.

VI.

The program was all around excellent. The way the instructors treated me was great because they didn't seem to think of us as any less than those students on campus. We were treated equally and that was great (Marshall & Andrews, 1991).

The Dual-Credit Boom in Illinois

One of the newest and largest educational movements in Illinois, as around the country, has been that of dual-credit enrollments for secondary school students. In a research study of the states 48 community colleges, Andrews (2000) reported a 240% growth over a two-year period in this program among the Illinois community colleges.

All 48 of the public community colleges responded to a statewide survey sent out in the summer of 2000 to determine how rapidly this program was expanding. The study also identified where the enrollment growth was being focused and identified the issues generated.

The colleges reported a total of 290 secondary schools participating in dual-credit programs during the 1999-2000 academic year. This number was up significantly from the 120 secondary schools participating two years previously.

Why the large increase?

The Illinois Community College Board (ICCB), with strong encouragement from the 48 community colleges, made an important funding change in its rules in 1996. It allowed the community

---

colleges to submit credit-hour grants through the ICCB for the first time even though secondary schools were continuing to claim the students as part of their average daily attendance.

In the 2000-2001 academic year the Illinois Community College Board went one step further and obtained state funding for each of the 48 colleges under a new program entitled *Accelerated College Enrollment Grant (ACE)*. This grant allowed college districts to receive monies at the rate of $55 per credit hour for credit hours generated in the dual-credit program. This tuition amount was not tied to any particular college's tuition or fee structure. It might have been close, however, to the state average for community college tuition for that year. The grant guidelines allowed colleges to decide whether to use the funds for full- or partial-coverage of the high school student's tuition and universal fees. The grant was developed to assist colleges to waive tuition and/or fees or reduce the tuition to the dual-credit students.

The grant funds were not adequate to cover the full-tuition amounts waived in the larger dual-credit programs. They did, however, provide a major improvement in the colleges' ability to reach out to more secondary school students and schools.

The ACE grant program was one more of the building blocks necessary to stabilize the funding and outreach efforts for the colleges. It has proved to be an important incentive in making the program accessible to all levels of social-economic students in the state of Illinois. The guidelines included:

> Accelerated College Enrollment Grant funding is intended to allow community colleges to expand their service to high school students desiring to take college-level classes prior to receiving their high school diploma. The grant is designed to assist high school students desiring to enroll in college-level classes to accelerate their college coursework (Illinois Community College Board,, June, 2001).

The dual-credit program had previously received an impetus in Illinois when an affordability study committee raised many issues regarding the cost and the length of time it was taking many students to earn a baccalaureate degree. One of their recommendations was to expand opportunities to secondary school students who could benefit from accelerated programs (State of Illinois, 1996).

The Illinois Community College Board Rules

A number of requirements are included in the dual-credit rules of the Illinois Community College Board (ICCB). They apply to those courses for dual-credit offered at the secondary school:

1. Courses offered by the college for high school students during the regular school day at the secondary school shall be college-level and shall meet the following requirements:
    A. State Laws and Regulations and Accreditation Standards. All state laws, ICCB regulations, accreditation standards specified by the North Central Association, and local college policies that apply to courses, instructional procedures and academic standards at the college apply to college-level courses offered by the college on campus, at off-campus sites, and at secondary schools. These policies, regulations, instructional procedures and academic standards apply to students, faculty and staff associated with these courses.
    B. Instructors. The instructors for these courses shall be selected, employed and evaluated by the community college. They shall be selected from full-time faculty and/or from adjunct faculty with appropriate credentials and demonstrated teaching competencies at the college level.
    C. Qualifications of Students. Students accepted for enrollment in college-level courses must have appropriate academic qualifications, a high level of motivation and adequate time to devote to studying a college-level course. The students shall meet all college criteria and follow all college procedures for enrolling in courses.
    D. Placement Testing and Prerequisites. Students enrolling in college-level courses must satisfy course placement tests or course prerequisites when applicable to

assure that they have the same qualifications and preparation as other college students.

E. Course Offerings. Courses shall be selected from transfer courses that have been articulated with senior institutions in Illinois or from the first-year courses in ICCB approved Associate in Applied Science Degree programs.

F. Course Requirements. The course outlines utilized for these courses shall be the same as for courses offered on campus and at other off-campus sites and shall contain the content articulated with colleges and universities in the state. Course prerequisites, descriptions, outlines, requirements, learning outcomes and methods of evaluating students shall be the same as for on-campus offerings.

G. Concurrent Credit. The determination of whether a college course is offered for concurrent high school and college credit shall be made at the secondary level, according to the school's policies and practices of the district.

The ICCB administrative rules provide a solid framework for Illinois community colleges. They spell out the possibility of both transfer and applied course offerings. The findings of the Illinois statewide study reported in this chapter bears out the success of the program being developed around the state.

The Dual-Credit Option for Students

Secondary school administrators and counselors are using the dual-credit option to challenge their juniors and seniors. The program carries college credit similar to the Advanced Placement (AP) program that a large number of the secondary schools have had in place for years.

This Illinois dual-credit program assures many talented students that they no longer have to wait to finish high school prior to starting college level work. Marshall and Andrews (1991) developed a program at Marquette High School in Illinois that allowed students the option of enrolling in one or two classes and earning from three to six credits a semester. These options were offered to juniors and seniors. Some students completed 24 credits during the two years and, by taking one summer session, some were able to start their first-full year of college as sophomores.

Dual-Credit Course Offerings

The Illinois system became comprehensive in the type of dual-credit to be offered to secondary schools and their students. Dual-credit classes were offered in three major areas: (1) *transfer courses* that lead to the baccalaureate degree; (2) *technical courses* that lead toward an Applied Associate Degree or a college certificate in the technical field; and (3) *vocational courses* that can also lead to the Applied Associate Degree or a technical certificate or act as a career orientation option.

Other students who have a special talent in art, computers, music, automotive, and other course areas are also enrolling in these programs across Illinois. The 2000 study in Illinois documented the following course options as being those most consistently offered during the 1999-2000 school year:

Most offered dual-credit courses for *Transfer* college credit:

English 101	22 colleges
History, U. S.	11 colleges
Psychology, Introduction	17 colleges
Calculus	10 colleges
Mathematics	15 colleges
Sociology, Introduction	7 colleges

Most offered dual-credit courses for *Technical* college credit:

Cisco Networking	13 colleges
Computer Information Systems	6 colleges
Mechanical Technology	9 colleges

Most offered dual-credit courses for *Vocational* college credit:

Automotive	14 colleges
Welding	4 colleges
Nursing assistant	4 colleges
Electronics Engineering Technology	3 colleges
Cosmetology	3 colleges

Over 80 courses were listed in the summary from the surveys received.

It appeared that the majority of the transfer classes were being offered at the high schools for honor students. A significant number of the colleges have opened their introductory classes in technology or vocational certificate and applied degree areas on the campus. A number of these are offered under the Tech Prep programs. The decrease in vocational offerings at the secondary school level has made the colleges' offer of having the technically and vocationally interested students come to campus an attractive one. Some students are integrated into existing class sections and others are in special sections of the courses set up to meet the time frame necessary for the secondary schools.

One Campus: Various Options

The following is a summary of how one rural campus has worked with a number of secondary schools to accommodate various needs for dual-credit. Dr. Jackie Davis, Dean of Instruction at Olney Central College (OCC), has seven high schools involved with the OCC dual-credit program. The courses, type of delivery, location, and high schools are outlined:

Course/Program	Delivery	Location	High School(s)
1. Industrial Maintenance	Classroom/Lab	Area Industry	Flora; North /Wayne North Clay; Clay City W. Richland H. S.'s
2. Collision Repair Tech.	Classroom/Lab	Campus	E. & W. Richland
3. Automotive Service	Classroom/Lab	Campus	E. & W. Richland
4. Cisco Networking	Classroom/Lab	Campus	E. & W. Richland
5. Web Designer Certif.	Classroom	High School	E. & W. Richland
6. Woodworking	Classroom/Lab	Campus	E. & W. Richland
7. Prin. of Economics	Classroom/H.S.	2-Way T.V.	Flora High School
8. Composition I & II	Classroom/H.S.	2-Way T. V.	Flora High School
9. Fundament. Speech	Classroom/H.S.	2-Way T. V.	Flora High School
10. Calculus I	Classroom/H.S.	High School	E. Richland H. S.
11. U. S. History I &II	Classroom/H.S.	High School	E. Richland H. S.
12. World Literature	Classroom/H.S.	High School	E. Richland H. S.

This is not the complete listing of the Olney Central College (OCC) course offerings. It does, however, show the various delivery systems that can be utilized by a college. Some of the courses are at the Hella Industry in Flora, Illinois. The industrial firm is central enough for five different high schools to send students to the Industrial Maintenance classes. The courses are held at the factory in their training classroom and the "live lab" of the production floor.

Collision Repair Technology, Automotive Service, CISCO, and Woodworking classes are offered on the college campus for the students from two high schools located one- and seven-miles from the college campus. The OCC full-time instructors teach these classes.

The four classes in Economics, Composition I and II, and Fundamentals of Speech are college transfer classes offered to Flora High School students (25 miles from campus). These classes are offered over the college and high school distance learning two-way interactive telecommunications system. These courses are taught by full-time teachers from the OCC campus. OCC students are in the college classroom at the same time. Calculus I, U. S. History I and II, World Literature, Psychology, Business Law I, and others are offered at the East Richland High School. These courses have been taught by high school teachers carefully selected as meeting the hiring qualification guidelines of the college district.

Quality Safeguards

All 48 community colleges were asked in the survey about their concerns relative to quality in the program. The top two responses mentioned were (1) testing to assure proper placement (and readiness) for courses; and (2) having faculty in the program meeting the basic qualifications and competencies required by the college to teach the dual-credit courses. In most cases the respondents mentioned that the same qualifications for full-time and part-time faculty were expected. Colleges used both full-time, part-time adjunct and secondary school qualified faculty in their programs.

Some of the other safeguards mentioned were: (1) course syllabuses being the same as courses offered on-campus; (2) use of the same textbooks as on-campus; (3) department chairs observing the classes once a semester; (4) secondary school counselor recommendations; and (5) student evaluations.

Program Outlook

Colleges were asked to make statements relative to the outlook in the future for this program. Most of the responses received were very positive and included, "a win-win program;" "here to stay;" "the senior year schedule will look more like a college schedule;" and "it offers stronger communications between secondary and post-secondary institutions."

Concerns

The concerns expressed centered around maintaining the quality and integrity of the classes taught for these secondary school students. Some concern was expressed that college faculty might lose some of their future enrollments. Transportation of students and faculty union concerns in both college and secondary schools were identified. High school students not being eligible for financial aid and resistance of some secondary schools to the program were the other concerns identified.

Summary

The prognosis for dual-degree programs in Illinois is positive. Growth is expected to continue in the coming years. The Illinois Community College Board has met many of the challenges to make sure this program can reach *all* social-economic levels of students in Illinois who can qualify. The ACE grants for tuition replacement (waiver) will go far in assuring equality of enrollment opportunity.

Quality issues generated the most concerns in the 2000 state-wide survey. They were being addressed to assure that dual-credit classes continue to be a highly acceptable program option for secondary school students, parents, secondary schools, and the universities and colleges where students will transfer their credits.

The Dual-Credit Phenomenon!

VII.

When Stacey R. Lee graduates from high school in this southeastern Illinois town next week, she'll have something her classmates are only beginning to contemplate: a college degree: (Teen Graduates from College, High School Just Weeks Apart, The Daily Times, 2001).

Outcomes of *Dual-Credit* for Students

The *Dual-Credit* program movement in American community colleges and secondary schools has expanded greatly in recent years. A number of options for secondary school juniors and seniors have, as a result, been developed through this program.

The importance of this program is being documented in states where it has existed for several years. It provides exceptional options to secondary schools wanting to offer challenging programs to their honor students as well as to students who need to explore career options and obtain technical and vocational background for the work force.

Outcomes for Students

The dual-credit program offers the following *outcomes* for secondary school students:

- An opportunity to enroll in college level course work while still in high school
- An opportunity to gain marketable technical or vocational skills not offered by the secondary school
- An opportunity to earn up to one semester of college credit

prior to (or immediately following) high school graduation
- An opportunity to earn up to one year of college work prior to (or immediately following) high school graduation
- An opportunity to earn up to two years of college work prior to (or immediately following) high school graduation

The following are outlines of *models* of dual-credit course options as they have evolved around the country:

Dual-Credit Model I

Obtaining one semester of college work concurrent with high school graduation.

A student would enroll in *one three-credit hour college course* per semester for each of the four semesters of the junior and senior year and one summer course *after* the junior *or* senior year: 15 credit hours = One Semester

Dual-Credit Model II

Obtaining one year of college work concurrent with high school graduation.

A student would enroll in *two three-credit hour college courses* per semester for each of the four semesters of the junior and senior year and two summer courses either *after* the junior *or* senior year: 30-32 credit hours = One Year

Dual-Credit Model III

Obtaining two years of college (Associate Degree) concurrent with high school graduation.

A student would enroll in *four or five college courses* per semester for each of the four semesters of the junior and senior year and two summer courses *after both* the junior *and* senior year: 60-64 credit hours = 2 Years (Associate Degree)

Technical and Vocational Dual-Credit Options

The next two dual-credit options models are in technical and vocational areas of the curriculum. These options are offered in a number of states although not as much has been reported about technical and vocational dual-credit programs. The need for articulation is important in those programs that fall under the *Tech-Prep* nationally recognized program. In the *Tech-Prep* programs students may earn college credit for introductory courses that have been articulated as being equivalent to the college courses in certificate or Applied Associate Degree programs at the community colleges.

Community colleges allow students to take introductory classes on the college campus as part of the dual-credit programs articulated with secondary schools. Many secondary schools have eliminated all of or major segments of their vocational programs due to lack of available faculty or due to the high costs involved in maintaining the programs. Students are bused or allowed to drive to college campuses for these options.

The following is a list of the technical and vocational course options that Andrews identified most often in the Illinois survey (2000) for dual-credit:

Technical

Cisco Networking; Mechanical Technology; Computer Information Systems; Computer Assisted Drafting; Electronics; Broadcasting; Networking; Introduction to the Internet; Information Processing; Telecommunications; Pharmacy Technology; Food Management and Emergency Technician (A total of 32 options were reported).

Vocational

Automotive Technology; Nursing Assistant; Welding; Electronics Engineering Technology; Cosmetology; Criminal Justice; Ornamental Horticulture; Machine Tool; Drafting; Culinary Arts;

Air Conditioning and Refrigeration; Banking; Electricity; Diesel Technology; Manufacturing Processes; and Gas Welding (A total of 29 options were reported).

Dual-Credit Model IV

> *Obtaining certification in a marketable technical area: i.e., CISCO Networking Specialist; Microsoft Certification, etc..*
>
> A student would enroll in one course per semester for each of four semesters of the junior or senior year, i.e.: 12 credit hours = Cisco Certification

Dual-Credit Model V

> *Obtaining coursework in technical or vocational classes at the high school or college that leads toward a certificate or technical Applied Associate Degree at a community college or into entry level jobs.*
>
> A student would be enrolled at the college or secondary school to obtain credit in some of the college's technical or vocational programs: Credit: Variable by program and/or as articulated between institutions

Student Options – Feedback

Student support for the above options can be sought through follow-up surveys and questionnaires upon completion of the program. The following comments relative to the *Fast Forward Program* of the University of North Carolina – Greensboro indicates students were most supportive of the dual-credit option afforded them during high school:

> The *Fast Forward Program* prepared me for college level work ... because of what I learned in *Fast Forward*, I did significantly better and placed into higher level classes.

I felt more motivated as a student.

I think *Fast Forward* is the best advanced learning program there is.

I am closer to graduating because of transferred credit.

I hope the program stays available at my high school and others. It's a terrific way to prepare for college. I love that my college credit wasn't dependent on one test!!!

The *Fast Forward Program* gave me the chance to get classes out of the way. I will be a junior in the fall, credit wise – but it will only be my second year of college. This is a great opportunity!

The above is a sampling of the type of feedback students across the country are giving to the dual-credit or concurrent enroll ment programs. Additional student responses are in the chapter on research follow-up on students (Chapter 8).

Making it work!

The dual-credit course option is a fast expanding program between community colleges, universities and secondary schools. In a number of states the universities and other four-year colleges are becoming a large part of the delivery of dual-credit options to students. Some important things need to happen to create a quality dual-credit program:

- *Agreements* between community colleges / universities and sec ondary schools need to be developed (See sample agreement in Appendix A);
- *Faculty* utilized in the dual-credit program need to be of the highest quality and meet the hiring requirements of the com munity college or university, use college syllabuses, and col lege textbooks, and have college support and evaluation pro cesses;

- *Students and parents* need to learn how these courses *articulate* into the community colleges and senior colleges degree programs or employment;
- *Counselors* at both the secondary school and college need to work together to assure students and parents of proper placement into the college coursework.

Personnel Involved

There are many persons involved in determining the outcomes of dual-credit experiences for students. Superintendents, principals, faculty, parents and counselors and Boards of Education are involved at the secondary school level.

At the college level college presidents, instructional leaders, faculty, counselors and Boards of Trustees each have roles in the program development and approval process.

Summary

Dual-credit programs offer many options for students across the country. The programs started out as a means of keeping secondary school students highly motivated during their last year or two of high school and has expanded significantly. Some states now allow students to obtain from one- to two-years of a college education while allowing those same courses to count as secondary school graduation requirements.

Dual-credit has been expanded in a number of states to allow students to enroll in technical and vocational programs. The *Tech-Prep* programs have allowed a significant number of students to earn college credits through their technical programs at the secondary schools. These are articulated programs usually developed between secondary schools and community colleges. Students may move into some of the more advanced technical and vocational classes at the college through this program. While the dual-credit program has been set up as another option to the *Advanced Placement* program that has been in existence for a number of years for secondary honor students, the dual-credit program has offered the additional option of taking dual-credit classes on the college campus as well as at the secondary school.

There has long been a fine line between high school honors courses offered to juniors and seniors and the first year of college courses in the same disciplines. The dual-credit option helps students to avoid duplication in curriculum while, at the same time, allowing them to move ahead with college work.

The Dual-Credit Phenomenon!

VIII.

Universities, colleges, and high schools should be encouraged to utilize the solid foundation of joint high school/college programs (Crossland, 1996).

Dual-Credit: *Local, State,* and *National* Research *Needs*

The majority of the dual-credit and concurrent enrollment programs are relatively new and expanding. It becomes very important to assess what is being accomplished as these new programs develop and impact many students and secondary school programs. What are the outcomes of the dual-credit programs around the country? What are the students saying after leaving the programs?

Other questions needing to be answered are: What has been the success in transferring dual-credit courses? Do the dual-credit students continue to enroll with the community colleges and universities offering the dual-credit courses they took in high school? What changes have been made by state educational agencies to improve their programs? Do early enrollment programs improve student motivation while still in high school? Is the program comparable to courses taken after enrolling full-time in college?

These are the type of questions that need to be researched and answered. Research provides the foundation for improving and

---

for assuring that the dual-credit programs are *quality* for students, parents, boards of education, college boards, state educational agencies and state legislators who are involved in deciding to fund these efforts. Research should also provide solid data for answering critics or doubters of the dual-credit programs. Kummer (2000) in her "*no*" article on dual-credit and the possibility that it might be a lesser quality program than the *Advanced Placement* program raised some of the issues that should be addressed. She questioned the quality of the dual-credit program in Arizona and suggested that the community colleges got involved in dual-credit mainly as a way to enhance their state funding.

It is important to hear from students that the dual-credit college transfer courses they took did, indeed, transfer to the college they attended after high school. While it may be of interest if the college they selected to attend is the same community college or senior college or university from which the dual-credit courses were taken during high school, it is more important to learn how other colleges and universities accepted their credits. It is even more of a concern to learn how well prepared the students were for the next level of study in the disciplines in which subsequent course work was taken.

Earlier studies: Illinois Valley Community College

There are few follow-up studies on dual-credit and concurrent enrollment programs recorded in the literature. Marshall and Andrews (1990) conducted a follow-up of students who had been enrolled at Marquette High School (MHS) in Ottawa, Illinois. Illinois Valley Community College cooperated with Marquette High School starting in 1985-86. This program, of college transfer course offerings, was made available to juniors and seniors. A total of six semester credits was one of the options possible for students in each of their last four semesters of high school for a total of 24 credit hours of college work. A second option was to have students enroll in one course each of the last four semesters and complete 12 semester hours by the time they graduated from MHS.

A follow-up of the students *grades* during the fall of 1986, spring of 1987, and fall of 1987 were compiled with the following grade distribution results: A's = 11 (4.8 percent); B's = 78 (34.8 percent); C's = 100 (44.6 percent); D's = 29 (12.9 percent); F's, incomplete, and withdrawals equaled 3 percent. The results were compared to the on-campus grades and found to be comparable (p. 49).

At commencement time, following two years of the MHS dual-credit program, high school seniors were asked for their response to the program (1986-1988). Some of their comments follow:

> The instructors were the best teachers I ever had. The program made me understand what college will be like. It took the fear out of me.

> Teachers were always willing to help and eager to teach. They didn't hold back material they didn't think we could handle. I've learned a great deal.

> The program was all around excellent. The way the instructors treated me was great because they didn't seem to think of us as any less than those students on campus. We were treated equally and that was great!

> They gave us a chance to experience college. The differences between high school and college really showed. The teachers are excellent (p. 49).

The students were next asked about how valuable the experience had been:

> Extremely valuable! They have given me enough hours, so that with summer courses, I can graduate (from college) in three years.

> It has been the most valuable learning experience that I received at MHS. I've gained a personal responsibility that one needs to excel in college (p. 49).

Impressions about IVCC

Students were asked to 'rank' their impressions about IVCC prior to and since taking courses in the dual-credit program. The change made with this group of students was dramatic. The pre-course scale was summarized at a 2.9 on a scale of five with five being the most positive of impressions. It was moved to a 4.2 average on the same scale of five as a result of having been dual-credit students.

Follow-up after enrolling in college

During the spring semester of 1988 the college sent out follow-up letters and surveys to 23 freshmen at their colleges and universities. Addresses were sought from parents and high school records. The date of the survey was ten months following graduation. Results were returned from 17 of the 23 (74%) students. One of the questions asked was, "If you are now enrolled in college, how well do you feel the IVCC coursework prepared you for your current program?" The number of responses to each of the five options were: excellent preparation (5); good preparation (10); fair preparation (2); less than adequate (0); poor preparation (0). Specific supportive comments were also received:

It really helped me to get ahead at school because I knew what to expect.

I feel it gave me an advantage over other freshmen here at school.

Two of the IVCC professors are the best I've had in my college career so far.

IVCC had the two most impacting professors I have had including my first semester at the University of Illinois.

The first two years of the MHS/IVCC program had an average of 35 graduates from the high school. They averaged 18 semester hours at the time of graduation from MHS. This was compared by the high school to student participation in the *Advanced Placement (AP)* program in prior years. Marshall and Andrews documented an average of three students per year with three AP credits being achieved. The school had a significant number of students in the AP program classes who had opted out of taking the exam at the end of the program (pp. 50-51).

Earlier studies: NIACC

A study of student learning in dual-credit courses offered at area high schools by Northern Iowa Area Community College was reported (Morrison 1998). It included the courses offered under the *Post-Secondary Enrollment Options (PSEO)* program. This program is offered to 11th and 12th grade students and a few 9th and 10th grade students who have been identified as talented and gifted. Morrison provided information on seven courses at various high schools starting in 1990-91:

1. 1990-91: Communication Skills I: Clear Lake School District

Methodology: Final writing papers from a traditional NIACC Communication Skills course (25 students) and the PSEO course (28 students from two sections) were collected. The names of the students and any other identifying characteristics were removed from the papers. The papers were shuffled and then submitted to Dr. James Zirnhelt, instructor and Division Chairperson, for assessment. Each paper was graded on a 0 to 4 scale on six separate criteria: purpose, content, organization, sentences, diction, and mechanics.

Findings: The null hypothesis that the means of the two groups were not significantly different at .05 probability was accepted.

Conclusion: Student writing outcomes are equal, as assessed by an evaluation of final writing papers.

2. 1990-91: General Psychology: Garner-Hayfield School District

Methodology: As the Garner-Hayfield students had an average 89th ITED percentile score, a matched pair methodology was employed. NIACC's psychology instructor, Kaye Young, matched Garner students with high ability traditional students in this college campus class. Outcomes were assessed on the basis of a 100 point multiple choice exam.

Findings: The Garner class mean was 84.35 with a standard deviation of 8.82. Campus mean was 84.82 with a standard deviation of 7.76. The t-test revealed no significant difference between the two groups at .05 probability.

Conclusion: Outcomes of the psychology classes as measured by a final exam are equal.

3. 1991-92: Criminal Law I: Mason City Community School District

Methodology: (This course was offered via telecommunications). The final test was utilized for the evaluation. Nineteen students were enrolled in the Mason City PSEO class while 21 students were enrolled in the NIACC on-campus class.

Findings: The mean of the Mason City High School group was 42.37 with a standard deviation of 4.425. This compared to the NIACC mean score of 45.62 with a standard deviation of 8.43. A t-test was utilized to test the null hypothesis that there was no significant difference between the means. The null hypothesis was accepted at .05 probability.

Conclusion: Outcomes for the telecommunications course, Criminal Law I, as measured by the final exams were not significantly different between the PSEO class and the NIACC on-campus class.

4. 1992-93: General Psychology: North Central Community School District

Methodology: A final exam was given to both the PSEO and the on campus NIACC classes. As group size varied, it was agreed

---

that the NIACC instructor would use the first 14 names in his grade book to compare with the 14 TAG (Talented and Gifted) students in the high school class.

Findings: The mean of the high school TAG class was higher, 3.53, than the mean of the traditional NIACC class, 3.03. A t-test was utilized to test the null hypothesis that there was no significant difference between the means. The null hypothesis was accepted at .02 probability.

Conclusion: Outcomes in General Psychology as measured by the final exam were not significantly different between the PSEO class and the NIACC on-campus class.

Three other classes were studied from 1993-94 with results published in the same fashion as the four classes analyzed above. Another General Psychology and two Business Statistics classes were processed through the same methodology with the result that Psychology and Business Statistics outcomes as measured by a final exam were equal in all three of these courses (pp. 1-3).

Morrison concluded, "PSEO is an important initiative for the college and its constituents. It provides excellent opportunities for high school students to be exposed to the academic rigors of college courses. Also, an analysis by Student Services demonstrates that we enroll a higher percentage of PSEO full-time students than those who have not enrolled in a PSEO course (p.3)"

At the conclusion of the data presented, Morrison stated the following:

- We are attracting a capable cohort of PSEO students.
- PSEO students enter the course with higher levels of ability than traditional college students on the NIACC campus.
- After ability levels are controlled, there are no significant dif ferences in PSEO and traditional students outcomes.

   The recommendation was made, "to continue and strengthen this important initiative (p.3)."

Syracuse University's Project Advance

One of the truly early pioneers in the dual-credit movement was Syracuse University with the *Project Advance* program. This program began in 1972, and in 1998-1999 there were 3,800 students enrolled. The students were enrolled in the states of New York, New Jersey, Massachusetts, Maine and Michigan.

The Syracuse program has over 400 teachers that they now certify as their adjunct faculty. They teach in 120 high schools in these five states. The success of their dual-credit students moving on to colleges or universities after high school was reported in 2001 as follows:

- 91% of Project Advance graduates received recognition for their courses
- 93% of these students report a g.p.a. of B or above through the four years of college
- 95% of these students recommended Syracuse University courses that were offered through Project Advance
- 92% of the teachers involved in Project Advance found their jobs more challenging (Syracuse University, p.1)

The Syracuse University model has provided much support over the years for other colleges and universities to establish successful models for their programs.

Southside Virginia Community College

The Southside Virginia Community College (SVCC) Office of Institutional Research found that 95.6 percent of the respondents to their follow-up survey of former dual-credit students reported they had enrolled in college following their dual enrollment experiences with SVCC (Mattox and Yancey, 1999). Their return rate was 29.2 percent from the 1,009 students who were sent questionnaires. These students were enrolled in 54 different institutions including 39 in Virginia. There were 183 in four-year colleges and 58 in two-year colleges. Forty-seven of the 58 were enrolled in SVCC. Other key research summary points were:

1. Respondents reported that 93.79% of their dual-enrollment credits did transfer successfully.
2. The respondents generally felt that dual enrollment classes were comparable to on-campus classes.
3. There was little change suggested for the program.
4. Respondents were nearly unanimous in making recommendations to continue the program.
5. The self-reported GPA at subsequent dual enrollment colleges was 2.991. These students had obtained a GPA of 3.135 in dual enrollment classes. This represented less than .2 of a grade point difference.
6. Transfer colleges, in reporting to SVCC, showed that 98.2% of the credits were accepted for transfer (p. 18).

Southside Virginia Community College found their report to be very supportive of their large rural dual enrollment program. It provided factual evidence that the SVCC dual enrollment students were well prepared for entering the senior institutions and for the academic requirements once they arrive there.

Student comments to specific questions follow:

1. What was the BEST thing about your dual enrollment experience?

Getting credit for classes so I wouldn't have to take them in college. High school gives more individual help in dual enrollment classes that you couldn't get in college.

My dual enrollment experience prepared me for college courses.

The credits that transferred put me ahead.

It really prepared me for the curriculum here at Lynchburg College.

It helped me prepare for college and meet expectations of professors; plus, I'll be graduated earlier.

Getting ahead for college. By my second semester I was a sophomore.

I didn't have to go through freshmen classes at Virginia Tech.

It influenced me a lot to go out for opportunities because some of my classmates regretted not taking it.

I think the best thing about dual enrollment is that I was able to take a whole year's worth of credits without paying.

2. What ONE thing would you suggest be changed?

More classes!

More lab work in science classes (we had one hour a week).

Nothing! Both the history and English classes I took were similar to those courses here at Virginia Tech.

Enforce the rule that dual enrollment classes are college classes regardless of the fact that high school students are taking them. Make no "high-school" exceptions.

Make them more intensive and more difficult. The only class that seemed to compete was my calculus class. In fact, I surpassed its requirement and upper level courses have been a breeze.

Offer both semesters of Chemistry and Biology so that students do not have to start with second semester once they reach college.

Sadly, I have to suggest that more independent reading be emphasized because that is all you do in college besides write papers.

I think the program is wonderful. Many of my friends envy the fact that I'm ahead.

This has been a sampling of the comments made by students from SVCC's program. The comments were both *pro* and *con* relative to the program. The *con* comments were overwhelmingly in the form of suggesting improvements.

Out of a number of success stories returned in a previous follow-up, SVCC chose to highlight the information reported by David Wilmouth, a Randolph-Henry High School (RHS) student in a campus newsletter (Hales, 1997). Mr. Wilmouth graduated *summa cum laude* from the College of William and Mary in chemistry. He reported having the highest grade point average out of the graduating class of 1119 students. He was also the outstanding chemistry student. When he returned his follow-up survey he was in his first year of graduate work in chemistry at Harvard University.

Mr. Wilmouth had accumulated 44 college credits by the time he graduated as valedictorian of his high school class. He reported, "of those SVCC classes, 41 hours transferred to William and Mary. I took dual enrollment classes during the 11th and 12th grades. The classes offer good insight into typical college classes and offer good preparation for college (p. 4)."

In summary, the SVCC students found the dual enrollment classes to be comparable to the on-campus college classes. They also were pleased that these courses provided both a head start on college and gave students a strong preparation for their subsequent college work. They made few recommendations for change in the program.

Washington's Running Start Program: Growth and Savings

In its 2001 report on the *Running Start* program, the Washington State Board of Community and Technical Colleges announced a total of 13,092 high school students were enrolled in *Running Start* during the 1999-2000 school year. This was a six percent increase over the previous year. From its first two years as a pilot program in five colleges (1990-1992) to the first full year in 1992-93 when it became a statewide program with 3,350 students, this program has continued to grow tremendously. This program enrolls 9% of the state's public high school students.

The state of Washington estimated a savings of $36.9 million during the 1999-2000 school year of this program. In addition, the students were reported to have saved $13.6 million in college tuition costs. This is summarized as a total savings of $50.5 million. The savings come because the taxpayers are paying only once to support *Running Start* students in courses offering both high school and college credit. Yoshiwara and Hanson (2001) point out that, "a student can achieve four years of education while the state only pays for two years (p. 3)."

Rend Lake College

In a relatively small follow-up survey (Kinsey, 2000) Rend Lake College (RLC) in Illinois, 15 previous dual-credit students responded. Six of the students continued their college at Rend Lake College and eight reported going to a wide variety of universities. One student reported not having gone on to college.

In response to the question, "Did you have any problems with transferring your RLC credits/courses?" the answers given were: Yes = 0; No = 12; and 3 did not respond. The second question asked, "How much time-to-completion of your college program will having had the RLC courses in high school save you?," brought the following responses: one semester = 6; one year = 2; other = 3.

Students were asked to rate the RLC course(s) taken in high school: Outstanding = 2; Very good = 6; Average (good) = 4; Below average = 0; No response = 3.

When asked, "How do the RLC course(s) you had in high school compare with courses you have had since then?" they answered as follows: RLC courses better = 2; RLC courses as good = 6; RLC courses not as good = 3; No response = 4.

Seven students indicated that taking RLC courses changed their perception of RLC:

> *Many people have said that RLC is an 'easy' school. After taking* classes there, I now realize what a good school it is.

> After seeing the similarities and differences between RLC and Southern Illinois University, I wish I had gone to RLC for my first two years.

> Great program. It was a nice transition.

> I was not as intimidated. It made it a smoother transition.

The former dual-credit students were asked to compare how they perceived RLC both before and after they took classes with the college:

Before	NR.	After	NR.
Excellent	= 0	Excellent	= 2
Good	= 4	Good	= 9
Fair	= 8	Fair	= 1
Poor	= 0	Poor	= 0

When asked, "Would you recommend dual-credit options like the program you participated in to other high school students?" the response was YES = 12; NO = 0. One respondent said, "I definitely recommend this program to each and every high school student who is eligible."

Virginia research concerns

A research report by Roesler (1992) identified some of the early concerns in the development of Virginia's dual-credit program. These concerns were coming from the public, the legislature, and four-year institutions. They were spelled out in the *Virginia Community College System Study of the Colleges' Operation of Dual-Credit Agreements with Public High Schools*:

> There are doubts and concerns about what the public school and community college partnerships are accomplishing with their dual-credit instruction. The individual colleges and the System need to collect and analyze student performance data, by courses and discipline. The public, therefore, should be informed about procedures (1) to determine which students are eligible for admission to dual credit courses, (2) to measure student achievement and verify that they have acquired knowledge and skills commensurate with college level instruction, and (3) to assess dual-credit students' subsequent academic achievement in non-dual-credit courses taken at the community colleges or the universities.

> Until we are able to report on whether or not students who have taken dual-credit instruction are as adequately prepared to do college level work as those who never took the dual-credit courses, the concerns about the effectiveness and quality of dual enrollment instruction will remain (p. 5).

Only 7 of the 17 colleges were found at that time to assess student outcomes. The conclusion was that, "each community college, without exception, should have a strategy for assessing student learning outcomes in dual-credit courses" (p. 9).

Washington's' Running Start Student Characteristics (2000)

The *Running Start* program in Washington conducts annual progress reports. Hanson (2000) found in the tenth year of the program that *Running State* students were continuing to perform well in (1) the two-year colleges and (2) in the universities.

Grade point averages were compared to other groups. In the two-year college group *Running Start* students had a 3.12 average while all of the regular two-year students averaged 2.99. In the University of Washington the g.p.a.'s were about 3.09 for both *Running Start* and regular freshmen entering the university.

The demographics for this year were similar to previous years:

- 59 percent of the students were female
- Over 15 percent were students of color
- The average credit load taken by the students was 9-11 credits per quarter
- 2 percent of students had disabilities
- A total of 42 percent worked part-time and 1 percent worked full-time
- Approximately 80 percent of the students were enrolled in academic courses

Savings. The *Running Start* program in 1999-2000 was analyzed showing savings to the taxpayers and parents for the year amounted to $37.12 million dollars. Approximately $24.6 million to the taxpayers and another $12.5 million in tuition charges were saved. There were 7299 full-time equivalent students served by the program in this year. In a previous study, 1995-96, Crossland reported the savings were $14.1 million for the Washington taxpayers and $6.6 million in tuition costs. This is due to the fact that the K-12 funds pay for student costs in both their high school and college course work.

University of Washington. A study of 88 *Running Start* students who entered the University of Washington in the fall of 1993 found that 40.9 percent (36 students) graduated at the end of four years. A comparison with other students showed that 31 percent of the regular students graduated in the same four years. Running Start graduates had achieved a 3.42 g.p.a. compared to the regular entering freshmen students who achieved a 3.14 g.p.a. (Hanson, p. 4).

During 1999-2000 the *University of Washington's Center for the Study of Capable Youth* made the following conclusion:

Students, on the whole seem very satisfied with the *Running Start* program and, more importantly for our purposes, satisfied with their own preparation for and progress in that program ... for them, the community college provided just the kind of learning environment that they had been craving (p.4).

In the 1995-1996 report Crossland (1996) identified that 89 percent of the *Running Start* students who were surveyed indicated that the experience was good enough that they would participate again.

This finding was similar to the one found by Crossland (1992) for the State Board for Community and Technical College. In this study both students and parents perceived the *Running Start* program as successful and acceptable.

Summary

Limited research studies have been conducted on dual-credit programs and outcomes up to this time. The success of students who have been enrolled in these programs was outlined. Students reported improved perceptions of the community colleges after being enrolled in dual-credit courses. Perceptions were even more positive after students enrolled in universities and had college level comparisons they could make between courses.

Success of transfer to subsequent colleges with little to no loss of credit was documented in several studies. Students were willing to promote the program to other students in the secondary schools. The quality of teaching in the programs was highlighted as being as *good as* or *better than* that received in subsequent classes in colleges by many of the respondents in the studies.

The arena of dual-credit research is wide open for colleges and graduate students to continue building the research base for this new and expanding program. Continued research will help colleges and secondary schools adjust their programs in order to obtain the highest quality the programs are capable of presenting students.

IX.

Dual enrollment works as an educational option. For the student ready for the challenge and independence of college, dual enrollment provides the luxury of acclimating to new college roles while remaining within the security of home, school and friends. At a pace that can differ for each individual student, dual-enrolled students can oscillate between the new and the familiar (McCarthy, 1999).

Summary...*Prognosis*

The dual-credit movement has taken the American community colleges and secondary schools by storm at the beginning of the 21st Century. It is likely to become one of the most significant educational reform movements since the growth of the community college movement in the last half of the 20th Century. A number of state universities and four-year colleges are involved in these programs and have developed some outstanding models.

Former research studies found over 30 states with legislation providing support and regulations for dual-credit programs. This author found dual-credit or dual enrollment programs existing in 48 states and programs being developed in the other two. Some were still at a very informal stage, with individual colleges and secondary schools working out arrangements to fit their needs, in an absence of any state procedures and/or laws. During a group discussion in late 2000 with Dr. Steven Crow, Executive Director of The Higher Learning Commission (North Central Association), he responded to a question on NCA's role with dual-credit that it might, indeed, be time to include dual-credit evaluation as part of their accreditation process. He was speaking with the *Counsel of Community College Presidents* of Illinois.

There are significant numbers of programs in states that provide the option for students to enroll in college campus courses *and/or* have the option to enroll in college courses offered at their home high schools.

In several other states, students must attend classes at the college campus. The equipment and space limitations of high school facilities for technical and vocational programs makes this necessary for a significant number of programs. Still other states resist the colleges hiring qualified secondary school faculty to teach the dual-credit courses on the secondary school campuses.

There are several arguments put forth for attending classes only on the college campus by some of the universities which are still debating whether or not to accept the dual-credit courses taught at high schools. One has been their promotion of the need for secondary school students to experience the college environment with regular college students. This argument is weakened, however, when one reviews the fact that some of these same universities offer secondary school students correspondence classes, and internet class options, which are carried out in isolation of any college or secondary school peer environment or, as in the case of AP classes, are offered only to a secondary-school-student group.

Teachers, selected from full-time and part-time college faculty, teach in the dual-credit programs. Secondary school teachers are also hired to teach college dual-credit courses in many high schools. Secondary school teachers are required, in the majority of the states, to hold the same minimum teaching credentials as the college faculty. In many states the Master's Degree with 18 hours in the subject field being taught is the minimum credential required. Some outstanding faculty, with fewer credentials, have been utilized in some states. The regional accrediting bodies and state community college requirements take precedent in establishing the credentials needed in a number of states.

The problems spelled out in Chapter V show what can happen when dual-credit programs grow so fast that the state regulating bodies have not kept pace with setting standards for key elements of the program. The state of Missouri is a state that has worked hard to reach consensus on what quality standards are needed for their dual-credit programs. It became paramount in Missouri that students and parents have a guarantee, before enrolling in the dual-credit program, that the dual-credit courses are acceptable at senior colleges and universities.

Transferability of credits and student success in Florida dual-credit programs were questioned of credits in a negative university research article also highlighted in Chapter V. The weak research presented in a university article motivated two large Florida community colleges to conduct their own follow-up research studies. Both colleges were able to document that their former dual-credit students were, indeed, doing very well at the senior colleges where they later enrolled. The state of Florida also conducted a system-wide study of former students from the dual-credit program and documented a high degree of student success across the state in universities and community colleges.

There has been limited research conducted and reported to date on what happens to dual-credit students. There are also limited follow-up studies documenting how students feel about their dual-credit experiences. Some studies were outlined in Chapter VII and provided data that was both positive and critical of dual-credit programs. Former dual-credit students were, for the most part, very positive about their experiences and successes following high school graduation. Most graduates of these programs urged the colleges to continue to offer the programs and thanked them for the opportunity they had received. The more critical students made suggestions on how to improve the dual-credit programs.

Individual colleges, state agencies, and university graduate research programs would find dual-credit and concurrent enrollment programs a very fertile ground on which to conduct follow-up studies and program evaluation. Some questions needing such research support are: What happens to students who are enrolled in the transfer, technical or vocational dual-credit programs? Do they enroll in the on-campus certificate or degree programs after high school? Does the program assist them in making a career choice? What do students think about the quality of the teaching in the dual-credit offerings? Does dual-credit save states and students money and shorten the time-to-degree? These are but a few of the questions that need research and follow-up studies.

Some critics have been quick to point out that colleges have entered into dual-credit for economic reasons. After working with dual-credit programs for over 17 years this author reports from personal experiences that economics are not a defining factor. These programs take significant work and time to properly administer.

They involve many meetings that bring administrators and faculty together from both types of institutions. They require policy decisions, and publicity, as well as meetings with parents, counselors, service clubs and organizations, and conducting research and follow-up. In addition, many colleges have waived or significantly reduced tuition for their dual-credit students. This has allowed enrollment of students from all social and economic classes.

Some critics have pointed to the dual funding that both the secondary schools and the colleges receive in a number of states. I have presented research and state responses to this question in various places throughout this book. What some may call "double-dipping" has often been just enough financial support to provide the incentive that has allowed the dual-credit programs to expand and accommodate students from all social and economic backgrounds.

The *Running Start* program in the state of Washington estimates dual-credit creates a savings of $50 million a year for the state and parents in terms of tuition and state apportionment costs. The state of Washington considers it is getting two years of education for the cost of one year or for a fraction of one year. Parents and students understand the savings made through the dual-credit program as do state governors and legislators.

In Illinois the Accelerated College Enrollment (ACE) grants replaced tuition for those colleges *waiving* or *reducing significantly* the tuition for enrollees. These funds are small compared to the tremendous cost savings that are being passed on to the state and to students and their parents from reducing time in college by a semester or year.

There is much work to be done in the years ahead to assure quality in the dual-credit experiences for students. The dual-credit program has improved the secondary school challenges and increased course options for thousands of high school juniors and seniors over the past few years. Secondary school administrators have reported to the author that having dual-credit courses has improved teaching within the participating high schools. Teachers in courses that prerequisite to dual-credit courses have a new challenge in preparing students for these college level courses.

With the growth being felt in the early years of the 21st Century the positive impacts of dual-credit will continue as new programs are offered. Enlightened state government and educational coordinating agencies can do much to improve on the delivery, expansion, and financial support available for schools offering dual-credit options and for those students enrolling in dual-credit programs.

This book has been written to provide the reader an overview of dual-credit and concurrent enrollment programs throughout America at the start of the 21st Century. The bibliography will provide a source for more in-depth information on tuition plans, student enrollment requirements, state funding support and other internal information from each of the states.

The Dual-Credit Phenomenon!

X. Bibliography

Andrews, H. A. "The Dual-Credit Explosion at Illinois' Community Colleges." *Community College Journal*, Dec. 2000 / Jan. 2001, pp. 12-16.

Andrews, H. A. "The Dual-Credit Explosion in Illinois Community Colleges." *Research Brief*, Olney, IL, 2000, pp. 1-4.

Andrews, H. A. "The Dual-Credit Movement in Community Colleges." *J. Staff, Program, & Organization Development*, 2000, *17*(4), pp. 201-206.

Andrews, H. A. & Marshall, R. P. "Challenging High School Honor Students with Community College Courses." *Community College Review*, 1991, *19*(1), pp. 47-51.

Andrews, H. A. & Marshall, R. P. "Challenge Students with College Work." *The School Administrator*, 1990, *11*(47), p. 35.

Atwell, C. & McLeod, M. *Performance of Dual Enrollment Students at UWF*. Memorandum from the Office of the Executive Vice President, Pensacola Junior College, to the Council of Institutional Affairs, Florida Community College System, Jan., 1994.

Basinger, J. "States Urged to Coordinate Public-School and College Systems." *The Chronicle of Higher Education*, *46*(46), July 21, 2000, p. A23.

Benbow, C. & Lupinski, D. *Intellectual Talent Development*. John Hopkins University Press, Baltimore, MD, 1996.

Bennett, W. J. *James Madison High School: A Curriculum for American Students*. Washington, DC: U. S. Department of Education, 1987.

Blackmore, J. D. *Committee to Study Affordability Report to Board of Higher Education*, State of Illinois, Board of Higher Education, Springfield, IL, 1994.

Boswell, K. *Building Bridges Not Barriers: Public Policies that Support K-16 Education*, Education Commission of the States, Denver, CO, Oct., 2000.

Brown, J. L. *The High School Partnership Program at Kansas City Kansas Community College.* Paper presented at the Annual International Conference of the National Institute for Staff and Organizational Development on Teaching Excellence and Conference of Administrators, Kansas City, KS, May 26, 1993.

Brody, L. "Dual Enrollment Programs: Part-time College for High School Students," *Imagine*, I, 1999, Jan./Feb., p. 25.

Carr, L. L. *Principles of Good Practice for Dual-Credit Programs*. Virginia Community College System, Richmond, VA, May, 1997, pp. 1-4.

Catron, R. K. "The Virginia Plan for Dual Enrollment: A Historical Perspective." *Inquiry*, *2*(1), Spring, 1998, pp. 13-21.

Cincinnati State Technical and Community College. *9th, 10th, 11th and 12 Grades Post-Secondary Enrollment Options as Provided for in Senate Bill 140*, Cincinnati, OH, 1999.

Community College Times. "National: Dual Enrollment Grows 36 Percent," Washington, DC, March 7, 2000, p. 6.

Connecticut Community College System. *Community-Technical College High School Partnerships Program.* Hartford, CT, 1987.

Crossland, R. *Running Start 1995-96 Annual Progress Report.* State Board for Community and Technical Colleges, Olympia, WA, 1997, pp. 3-5.

Crossland, R. *Running Start 1996 Survey Report.* State Board for Community and Technical Colleges, Olympia, WA, 1996, p. 6.

Davis, J., Marshall, R. & Andrews, H. A. "Outcomes of Dual-Credit for Students." *Research Brief,* Olney, IL, 2000, p. 1-2.

Education Commission of the States. *Post-secondary Options/Dual Enrollment,* ECS Clearinghouse, Denver, CO, 1997.

Fincher-Ford, M. *High School Students Earning College Credit: A Guide to Creating Dual-Credit Programs*, Thousand Oaks, CA, Corwin Press, 1997.

Florida Community College System. *Putting Minds to Work.* Bureau of Financial and Business Services, Tallahassee, FL, 2000.

Florida State Board of Community Colleges. *High School and Community College Dual Enrollment Issues of Rigor and Transferability, A Level I Review,* Tallahassee, FL, Jan., 1997.

Gerber, C. *High School College Brief.* Supplement to *AACJC letter*, no. 242, May 19, 1987.

Girardi, A. G. & Stein, R. B. *State Dual-Credit Policy and Its Implications for Community Colleges: Lessons from Missouri for the 21st Century.* Missouri Coordinating Board for Higher Education, Jefferson City, MO, 2000.

Hales, C. "Harvard Grad Student Attended SVCC Dual Program." *Connections: SVCC Newsletter*. Alberta, VA, Spring, 4, 1997.

Hanson, S. Z. *Running Start 1999-2000 Annual Progress Report*. State Board for Community and Technical Colleges, Olympia, WA, 2000, 3-5.

Idaho State Board of Education. *Governing Policies and Procedures: Section 111 Post-secondary Affairs; Subsection Y: Accelerated Learning Programs*, Feb., 2000, pp. HI-92-94.

Illinois Community College Board. "Accelerated College Enrollment Grant (ACE)," *Policy Guidelines for Restricted Grant Expenditures and Reporting, Fiscal Year 2001*, June 16, 2000.

Illinois Community College Board. "Accelerated College Enrollment Grant (ACE)," *Policy Guidelines for Restricted Grant Expenditures and Reporting, Fiscal Year 2002*, June, 2001.

Illinois Community College Board. *Administrative Rules of the Illinois Community College Board*, Springfield, IL, 1999, pp. 63-64.

Iowa Department of Education. *Post-Secondary Enrollment Act. Iowa Code*, Des Moines, IA, 1999.

Jones, E. & Southern, T. *Acceleration of Gifted Children*, Teachers College Press, New York, NY, 1989.

Joyce, M. "Report from the dual enrollment front; Durango, Colorado: Catapult' to graduation." *Community College Times*, Dec. 12, 2000, p. 7.

Kansas Board of Regions. *Guidelines for Concurrent Enrollment of High School Students in Community College Courses: Kansas Challenge to Secondary School Pupils Act*, K.S.A., 1993 Supp. 72-lIa0I through 72KS.,1993.

Kentucky Community and Technical College System. *Dual-Credit Guidelines.* Council on Postsecondary Education 2-1132, Frankfort, KY, 2000-2001.

Kinsey, N. "Rend Lake College Dual Enrollment Survey." *Institutional Research.* Rend Lake College, Ina, IL, Fall, 2000.

Knight W. E. *Early Admission Students Study.* Kent State University, OH., April, 1992.

Kronholz, J. "Academic Question: Why Has Senior Year of High School Lost Its Purpose for Many?" *The Wall Street Journal,* March 23, 1999, p. 83.

Kummer, L. "High standards have been an unfortunate casualty. Point of View: Is it dual enrollment--or double vision?" *Community College Times, 10*(23), Nov. 14, 2000.

Lambert, L. M., & Mercurio, J. A. "Making Decisions: College Credits Earned In High School." *The Journal of College Admissions,* 1986, Spring, pp. 28-32.

Legg, S. "Utilization of Accelerated Credit: University of Florida." *Research Report,* Office of Instructional Resources, University of Florida, Gainesville, FL, 1993.

Lords, E. "New Efforts at Community Colleges Focus on Underachieving Teens." *The Chronicle of Higher Education,* June 30, 2000, p. A45.

Maine Technical College. "System Tuition Waiver and Reduction Program for Qualified High School Students," *Procedures Manual, Academic Affairs,* Section 310. Augusta, ME, 2001.

Mattox, R. & Yancey, A. *Southside Virginia Community College Dual Enrollment Program, 1995-96 and 1996-97: Survey Results from Participants,* Office of Institutional Research, Keysville, VA, 1999.

Marshall, R. P., & Andrews, H. A. "Challenging High School Honor Students with Community College Courses." *Community College Review, 19*(1), 1991, pp. 47-51.

McCarthy, C. R. "Dual-Enrollment Programs: Legislation Helps High School Students Enroll in College Courses," *Journal of Secondary Gifted Education*, Fall, 1999, *11*(1), pp. 24-32.

Mees, R. *Dual-Credit Courses: Survey Information from Selected Community Colleges in Illinois.* John A. Logan College, Carterville, IL, 1999.

Michigan Department of Education. *Post-secondary Enrollment Options Act Update Newsletter*, August 31, 1999.

Minnesota Office of the Legislative Auditor. *Post-secondary Enrollment Options Program.* St. Paul: Minnesota Office of the Legislative Auditor, 1996.

Morrison, M. C. *NIACC Post-Secondary Enrollment Options Courses: Quality Control Synopsis*, Northern Iowa Area Community College, Mason City, IA, October 22, 1998.

Nespoli, L. A. "New Jersey's Dual Admissions Program. *Community College Journal, 67*(4), Feb./Mar., 1997, pp. 22-26.

New Hampshire Community Technical College System. *The Running Start Program: A Higher Education Program for High School Students.* Concord, NH, Fall, 1999, pp. 1-2.

New Jersey Commission on Higher Education. *Survey Findings: College Courses Offered in New Jersey High Schools.* Trenton, NJ, March, 1997.

New Mexico State Board of Education and New Mexico Commission on Higher Education. *New Mexico Policies Governing Concurrent Enrollment of Secondary Students at Post-secondary Institutions.* Santa Fe, NM, 1990.

North Dakota University System. *The Delivery of Dual-Credit College Courses by the North Dakota University System,* Bismarck, ND, May 27, 1999, pp. 16.

Oregon University System. *Oregon Early Options Study,* Office of Academic Affairs, Eugene, OR, Jan. 20, 1999.

Osborne, D., & Gaebler, T. *Reinventing Government: How the Entrepreneurial Spirit is Transforming the Public Sector.* Reading, MA, Addison Wesley, 1992.

Puyear, D. *Concurrent and Dual Enrollment of High School Students in Arizona Community Colleges: A Status Report.* Arizona State Board for Community Colleges, Phoenix, AZ, Aug. 7, 1998.

Reisberg, L. "Some Professors Question Programs that Allow High School Students to Earn College Credits." *The Chronicle of Higher Education,* June 26, 1998, pp. A39-40.

Roesler, Elmo D. *Virginia Community College System Study of the Colleges Operation of Dual-Credit Agreements with Public High Schools,* May 18 to September 8, 1992, Virginia State Department of Community Colleges, Richmond, Sept., 1992.

Samson, S. M. *Statutory Program for High School Students Enrolling at Institutions of Higher Education.* Colorado Commission on Higher Education, Aug. 21, 1998.

Schoolcraft College. "Opportunities for High School Students at Schoolcraft College," *Enrollment Brief,* Livonia, MI, 1998.

South Carolina Board for Technical and Comprehensive Education: Division of Academic Affairs and Technology State Board for Technical and Comprehensive Education. *Procedure 3-6-101: Procedures for Developing Course and Program Articulation Between Secondary Schools and Technical Colleges,* Columbia, SC, pp. 1-3.

Southside Virginia Community College. *Dual Enrollment Survey 1995-96 and 1996-97.* Office of Institutional Research, Keysville, VA, 1999.

State Board of Directors for Community Colleges of Arizona. *Special Admission of Students Under Age Eighteen: Enrollment Information Reports 15-1821*, Phoenix, AZ, 1999.

State of Illinois, Board of Higher Education. *Report of the Committee to Study Affordability,* Springfield, IL, November 9, 1994.

State of Illinois, Board of Higher Education. *Status Report on Implementation of Policies Recommended by The Committee to Study Affordability,* Springfield, IL, March 5, 1996.

Syracuse University. *SUPA Online: Research,* Syracuse, NY, http://supa.syr.edu/SupaOnline/General/FactSheet.htm, 2001.

Teen Graduates from College, High School Just Weeks Apart. The Daily Times, Ottawa, IL, AP Story, May 15, 2001, p. 7.

Texas Higher Education Coordinating Board. *Program Development in Public Community/Junior College Districts and Technical Colleges (Chapter 9); Subchapter H., Partnerships Between Secondary Schools and Public Two-Year Associate Degree-Granting Institutions*, Austin, TX, Oct., 1998, pp. .1-5.

The Commonwealth of Massachusetts, Department of Education. *The Massachusetts Dual-Enrollment Program.* Malden, MA, 1999, pp. 1-3.

University of Alaska. *Advance! A Program for High School Students. What's In It For Me?* Anchorage, AK: advance@uaa.alaska.edu/advance/forme.html, 2001.

Utah System of Higher Education. *Concurrent Enrollment, R-165.,* Salt Lake City, UT, Revised, April, 2000.

Windham, K. P. *Dual Enrollment Is Alive and Well in Florida's Community College System,* Tallahassee: State Board of Community Colleges, 1997.

Windham, K. P. "Follow-up of Dual Enrollment Students." *Inhouse Research Report,* Tallahassee Community College, Tallahassee, FL, 1994.

Wyoming Community College Commission. *Wyoming Post-secondary Education Options Program (WPEOP),* Laramie, WY, Sept., 1998.

Yoshiwara, J. & Hanson, S. *Running Start: A progress report from the State Board for Community and Technical Colleges,* Washington State Board of Community and Technical Colleges, Olympia, WA, Jan., 2001.

The Dual-Credit Phenomenon!

Appendix A

Illinois Eastern Community Colleges District 529 Dual-Credit Agreement

STATEMENT OF AGREEMENT

The Board of Trustees of Illinois Eastern Community Colleges District 529 and the Board of Education for [high school district] agree to enter into a partnership to provide dual-credit courses for academic and occupational courses that will be accessible and beneficial to high school students within the boundaries of the Illinois Eastern Community Colleges District. This agreement shall become effective on [date].

II.   STATEMENT OF PURPOSE

Dual-credit courses expand student access to affordable higher education, provide challenging academic and occupational experiences to qualified high school students during their junior and senior years, and reduce the costs of a college education for students and their families. Successful completion of transfer courses will enable students to simultaneously earn college credit transferable to two- and four-year colleges and universities and to satisfy high school graduation requirements. Successful completion of occupational courses will allow students to simultaneously earn college credits, to satisfy high school graduation requirements, and to assist in the transition to the community college or job opportunities and careers. Dual-credit courses are important transitional links in the Illinois Education-to-Careers System for young people moving from secondary schools to colleges and universities and high-skill, high-wage careers.

I.   GUIDELINES

A. Dual-credit courses are governed by the policies and regulations of the Illinois Community College Board, the Illinois State Board of Education, the North Central Association, and the policies and standards of Illinois Eastern Community Colleges and the [high school board of education]. These policies, regulations, and standards apply to students, faculty, staff, instructional procedures, academic standards, and course offerings, whether courses are offered at the college campus, at off-campus sites, including distance learning and Internet, or at secondary schools.

B. The Illinois Eastern community college and the high school will jointly select dual-credit courses in both transfer and occupational areas.   Transfer courses offered for dual-credit should be articulated with Illinois colleges and universities. Occupational courses offered for dual-credit should be first-year courses in ICCB approved Associate in Applied Science Degree and certificate programs.

C. Students enrolling in dual-credit courses must satisfy course placement tests or course prerequisites when applicable.

D. High school students who wish to enroll in dual-credit courses must be recommended and approved by their high school counselor and principal.

E. Academic advising services and course registration assistance will be provided jointly by the Illinois Eastern community college and the high school.

F. Matters of student discipline will be handled cooperatively between the Illinois Eastern community college and the high school.

G. Tuition for high school students who enroll in dual-credit courses will be based upon the following:

　1.   Tuition is waived for students for day (regular school

day) courses taught at either the high school or community college.

2.   Students will pay regular tuition rates for night classes (any class after 3:00 p.m.) or summer classes. Note: High school students enrolled in dual-credit courses are not eligible for state or federal financial assistance.

A. A dual-credit course will be identified on the college transcript in the standard format and will not be identified as dual-credit course.

B. Faculty teaching dual-credit courses will satisfy the Illinois State Board of Education requirements and the educational and professional standards and requirements of the North Central Association, the Illinois Community College Board, Illinois Eastern Community Colleges District, and the [high school].

C. The Illinois Eastern community college and the [high school] will jointly supervise faculty teaching dual-credit courses. Full time high school faculty members who teach dual-credit courses as part of their regular teaching assignment will not receive additional compensation. Illinois Eastern community college part-time and full-time faculty who teach dual-credit courses, will be compensated according to the policy approved by the IECC Board of Trustees.

D. Dual-credit courses offered during the regular school day shall have equipment and classroom/laboratory space provided by the host site at no charge to the other institution.

E. The Illinois Eastern community college and the [high school] will jointly conduct monitoring and evaluation of dual-credit courses.

F. There is a minimum enrollment of eight (8) students for dual-credit courses.

G. Consultation and mutual agreement with the CEO of the Illinois Eastern Community Colleges District and the Superintendent of the Unit School District, or their designees, may address items not covered in this agreement.

O. This agreement shall remain in effect until cancelled by official action by either the Board of Education or the Illinois Eastern Community Colleges Board of Trustees or by notice of the Superintendent of Schools or the CEO of Illinois Eastern Community Colleges of their intent to cancel this agreement.

I. BOARD APPROVAL

The Board of Trustees of Illinois Eastern Community Colleges District #529

By:_____
<pre>
              President   Date
              [Community Unit District # Board of Education]
</pre>

By:_____
<pre>
              Superintendent   Date
</pre>

dual credit district agreement

Appendix B

Marquette High School Special Graduate

Survey from I.V.C.C.

You were part of a very special program during your last two years at Marquette High School in Ottawa, Illinois. We are *conducting a survey to find out how important the "dual-credit" program from IVCC was for you.* Your answers will be treated confidentially. This type of program is expanding throughout Illinois now and your responses will help us understand better how the dual-credit program is helping students. *Please help!*

Questions:

1. Name _____

2. Year Graduated from MHS_____

3. ___ How many college credits did you get from IVCC during your last two years of high school?

4. _____What college did you attend immediately after graduating from MHS?

5. _____What college did you transfer to from IVCC (if IVCC is the college listed in Q. 4?)

6. ____How many of the credits (in question 3) did the college/ university accept from the IVCC/MHS program?

7. ___Yes ___No Did you have any problems with transferring any of the courses from IVCC?

   Comments:

8. If "yes" was checked in #7, which course(s) were a problem for transfer?_____

9. How do you rate the faculty that the IVCC program brought to MHS for you?
   ____A. Outstanding; ___B. Very Good; ___C. Average (good); ___D. Below Average

Please comment here on any answer you checked in question 9:
_____

10. How do you feel about having "dual credit" programs for juniors and seniors in high school?

11. How much time in attending college will having the IVCC program at MHS save you?
    A. One semester____; B. One year____; C. Other_____

12. How did the instructors brought to MHS for dual-credit from IVCC compare to the instructors you have had at the university since?____A. Better; ____B. As good; _____C. Worse

    Comments:_____

13. Did the dual-credit program from IVCC keep you challenged during high school __Yes; ___No

    Comments:_____

14. What was most valuable in the IVCC dual-credit program for you?_____
    _____
    _____

15. Did the dual-credit program _change your image about IVCC_?
    ___Yes; ___No
    A. If you checked _'yes'_ please indicate _in what way_? (examples: more respect for it; tougher than I thought; not as good, etc.)_____

    _____

B. Give your best _rating_ of what you thought about IVCC _before_ and _after_ being part of the dual-credit program:
   Before (Excellent = 1 to poor = 5) 1, 2, 3, 4, 5 (circle one)

   After (Excellent = 1 to poor = 5) 1, 2, 3, 4, 5 (circle one)

       Use return postage-paid envelope and Mail to:
              Dr. Robert Marshall
              Vice President of Students
              IVCC
              Oglesby, IL 61348

   THANK YOU VERY MUCH FOR YOUR RESPONSES

The Dual-Credit Phenomenon!